Stewart
Pla

Northern Star, Heavenly Bodies, Pentecost

Northern Star. 'His best play – by far . . . a fine Irish play by any standards. Parker speaks to the present through the past, using comedy, satire, parody and a seriousness that is nonetheless deadly for its being lightly drawn . . . It is played around the last seven years of Henry Joy McCracken's life, each age played in a marvellously funny pastiche of seven Irish authors . . . Seldom has Irish history been so provocatively or so entertainingly drawn on the stage.' *Irish Times*

'Compelling . . . intellectually absorbing in the perspectives it opens up and the insights it provides. The approach is inventive to a high degree and the writing has a marvellously imaginative sweep to it as it ranges from high literary excellence to comic parodies of Synge, O'Casey, Wilde and others. It is a remarkably stimulating play and, given its modern relevance, it has a tragic core of unlearned lessons.' *Irish Independent*

'Elegant, witty and moving . . . a remarkable virtuoso achievement.' *Observer*

Heavenly Bodies: 'An undoubted talent for pungent dialogue . . . The colourful, rather Balzacian story of Boucicault is carried by excerpts from his own works, variously light comic or melodramatic, which are introduced to him after his death in New York by the fantastical figure of Johnny Patterson, the "Irish Singing Clown" who was kicked to death while singing of Irish unity.' *The Times*

Pentecost: 'What makes it an extraordinary play is how much of Belfast and of Northern Ireland Parker manages to put on the stage: the politics, the religion, the tension between residents and exiles and, above all, the idea of a city and country haunted by its past and forever fuelled by a righteous anger. What makes the play so moving is Parker's burning conviction that recrimination is not enough . . . what animates it is Parker's own immense generosity of spirit and passionate belief that what unites us as human beings is infinitely more important than what divides us.' *Guardian*

'Exhilarating energy and mordant humour . . . The characters are beautifully drawn and the dialogue between the ill-assorted members of this uneasy household crackles with a rare wit and passion . . . Fine and moving.' *Daily Telegraph*

The volume is introduced by Stephen Rea, actor and director, with a foreword by Stewart Parker.

Stewart Parker was born in Belfast in 1941. During the early sixties at Queen's University he was active in a group of young writers which included Seamus Heaney and Bernard Mac Laverty. His first stage play *Spokesong* (1975) won him the 1976 *Evening Standard* Most Promising Playwright Award and his TV drama *I'm a Dreamer, Montreal* (1979) won the Ewart-Biggs Memorial Prize. His stage plays include *Catchpenny Twist* (1977), *Nightshade* (1980), *Pratt's Fall* (1983), *Northern Star* (1984), *Heavenly Bodies* (1986) and *Pentecost* (1987), which won the Harvey's Irish Theatre Award. He died in London in 1988.

STEWART PARKER PLAYS: 1
(Spokesong, Catchpenny Twist, Nightshade, Pratt's Fall)

STEWART PARKER

Plays: 2

Northern Star
Heavenly Bodies
Pentecost

introduced by Stephen Rea
with a foreword by Stewart Parker

Methuen Drama

METHUEN CONTEMPORARY DRAMA

This collection first published in the United Kingdom in 2000
by Methuen Publishing Limited
215 Vauxhall Bridge Road, London SW1V 1EJ

www.methuen.co.uk

Northern Star, Heavenly Bodies and *Pentecost* first published in Great Britain in 1989
by Oberon Books Ltd as *Three Plays For Ireland*
Copyright © 1989 by the Estate of Stewart Parker
Foreword copyright © 1989 by Stewart Parker
Introduction copyright © 2000 by Stephen Rea

The right of the author to be identified as the author of these works has been asserted
by him in accordance with the Copyright, Designs and Patents Act, 1988

ISBN 0 413 74350 0

Methuen Publishing Ltd reg. number 3543167

A CIP catalogue record for this book
is available at the British Library

Typeset by Deltatype Ltd, Birkenhead, Merseyside
Transferred to digital printing 2002

Caution

All rights whatsoever in these plays are strictly reserved. Applications
for performance etc., should be made, before rehearsals begin, to Alexandra Cann
Representation, 12 Abingdon Road, London W8 6AF. No performance may be given
unless a licence has been obtained.

Contents

For
Lynne Parker

Stewart Parker
Chronology

1975   *The Iceberg*, BBC Radio Ulster
       Spokesong, John Player Theatre, Dublin Theatre
       Festival

1976   *Spokesong*, King's Head Theatre, Islington, London
       The Actress and the Bishop (one act), King's Head
       Theatre, Islington

1977   *Spokesong*, Vaudeville Theatre, London; wins
       Evening Standard Most Promising Playwright Award
       I'm a Dreamer, Montreal, BBC Radio 4
       Catchpenny Twist, Peacock (Abbey) Theatre,
       Dublin, and BBC Play for Today

1978   *Spokesong*, Long Wharf Theatre, New Haven,
       Connecticut
       Kingdom Come (musical), King's Head Theatre,
       Islington

1979   *Spokesong*, Circle in the Square Theatre, New
       York
       I'm a Dreamer, Montreal, Thames Television; wins
       Ewart-Biggs Prize
       Kamikaze Ground Staff Reunion Dinner, BBC Radio 3

1980   *Nightshade*, Peacock (Abbey) Theatre, Dublin
       Kamikaze Ground Staff Reunion Dinner wins Giles
       Cooper Award

1981   *Kamikaze Ground Staff Reunion Dinner*, BBC TV
       Iris in the Traffic, Ruby in the Rain, BBC TV

1982   *Joyce in June*, BBC TV

1983   *Pratt's Fall*, Tron Theatre, Glasgow

1984   *Northern Star*, Lyric Players Theatre, Belfast
       Blue Money, London Weekend Television film (US
       video)

1985   *The Traveller*, BBC Radio 3
       Radio Pictures, BBC TV

1986   *Heavenly Bodies*, Birmingham Repertory Theatre

Introduction

The vacuum in Irish theatre created by the death of
Stewart Parker in 1988 has expanded rather than
contracted; I am more aware than ever now that we are
still indebted to him and, further, that the debt has only
begun to be repaid. When I first met him in the 1960s
at Queen's University, Belfast, his theatrical instinct was
already highly developed. He knew how to teach others
even then, in a wholly unobtrusive yet practical way.
This was indeed to remain a feature of his own work. It
has an element that is didactic in its effect although it
does not have in its tone or its texture any sermonising
or wisely avuncular address. I remember him teaching
me how to laugh on stage, always an embarrassing task
for a young actor. 'Expel all the air from your lungs,' he
would say, 'then try to make a sound.' It was true. The
dry little cachinnation that I produced did, amazingly,
sound like a laugh. In a larger sense, he could illuminate
the limitations of certain kinds of theatre – that of social
realism, for instance – simply by reminding one that
'Nothing happens to a character after a play. When the
play is over, the character ceases to exist.' What I began
to learn about Stewart in those days was his precocious
awareness of where he wished to situate himself in
relation to the various theatrical traditions in which he
was already so deeply read. Although I do not wish to
make the choice sound overly self-conscious, I believe
nevertheless that a degree of self-consciousness was an
important feature of it. He chose to see himself as a
member of the community of dramatists that constitute
the Irish, or the Anglo-Irish tradition. It was an
important but also a difficult choice. In one sense, it was
a decision in favour of a theatre of ideas, but a theatre
that had always had a highly oblique relation to the
world of the metropolitan intellectual. The obliquity of
that relation manifests itself most famously in its wit and

that wit is both so cerebral and at times so surreal that
it makes the conventions of social realism seem inflexible
and predictable.

However, Stewart's unavoidable preoccupation with
the travails of the North of Ireland seemed to most
people to doom him to precisely those conventions; for
anything that did not smack of 'realism', of the 'this-is-
how-it-is' school, could in those days especially be
deemed to be in some sense disengaged from the
actuality of the situation. But Stewart found within that
Anglo-Irish tradition examples of the ways in which the
application of intelligence to a political situation could be
both liberating and revelatory. The dramatist and
novelist Thomas Kilroy has summarised this capacity of
the Anglo-Irish drama by what he calls its 'creative
distancing', its 'cool remove', and its celebration of the
'intelligence of the playwrights themselves, usually in the
form of wit and verbal elegance, but often in the
dramatising of ideas'.

Stewart has this eloquence, wit and the accompanying
obliquities. When did shipyard-workers achieve the kind
of eloquence we find in Danny and Hugh of *The Iceberg*?
Who but Stewart would have conceived of the sinking of
the *Titanic* as a ghost story, exposing social injustice,
class warfare and inaugurating thereby a debate on the
condition of Ireland? Equally, it seems characteristic of
Stewart's resourcefulness that he should transmute the
old Irish legend of Deirdre of the Sorrows, much
represented on the Irish stage during the Revival, into a
TV serial, *Lost Belongings*, wherein the tragic element of
the original story was retained but also re-realized both
for modern conditions and via the contemporary
medium. *Joyce in June*, a play for television, is another
example of Stewart's agility in recycling cultural
materials, including cultural clichés, for comic effect and
yet to serious and sometimes scathing purpose.

However, it is in *Northern Star* (1984) and *Pentecost*
(1987) that Stewart's career as a dramatist achieves its

most complex and satisfactory articulation. In *Northern Star* his engagement with Anglo-Irish drama from Farquhar to the present day is interwoven with his equally powerful preoccupation with the specifically Protestant republican and radical tradition of Belfast. The result is a work in which the political and the cultural are simultaneously represented as aspects of civil society that are, properly speaking, inseparable but that can, to their mutual detriment, become separated and then distorted as distinct modes of imagining. Sectarian prejudice produces sectarianised histories. Stewart himself declared in an article he wrote in 1985: 'I see no point in writing a "plea" for unity between prods and taigs. What use has piety been? I can only see a point in actually embodying that unity, practising that inclusiveness, in an artistic image; creating it as an act of the imagination, postulating it before an audience.' The search for such an image of unity, with its faint Yeatsian overtones of 'unity of being', and with its self-conscious use of the heavily charged word 'unity', is central to his most mature work.

The crux of the political weight and importance of Stewart's work lies here. In producing his image of 'unity' he could be said to be offering a kind of solution to the otherwise divided and sectarianised situation of Northern Ireland. On the other hand, such a postulated unity could be less benignly described as a wished-for alternative to the actualities of division, as a species of liberal humanism which is seeking to produce a set of universal values in despite of and in face of sectarianism and injustice. There is nothing ignoble in this, of course. But it is not necessarily a unity that derives from actualities. It is simply imported to replace them.

However it is in *Pentecost* that Stewart actually asserts this humanism with an unprecedented vigour. Beside the squalor of the death, destruction and provincial bitterness of the North, he places an ideal of the fully human, the fully realised life. In effect, he does not imagine for this desolate society a specific future. What he did in those particularly dark days was to imagine the possibility of a future at all. That was and is a memorable achievement. It is also true that Stewart Parker was the first Northern writer to produce such a vision of a harmonious possibility on the other side of violence. For that, and for his panache and style, for the fact that he restored to theatre a moral as well as a political dimension while adapting to the technical demands of the contemporary stage and media, he will always be remembered both with affection and with admiration.

Stephen Rea
1999

Foreword

I

Ancestral voices prophesy and bicker, and the ghosts of your own time and birthplace wrestle and dance, in any play you choose to write – but most obviously when it actually is a history play.

The three history plays in this volume were conceived and written, in consecutive order, between 1983 and 1987, as a common enterprise. Trilogy, however, may be too strong a word for them. Triptych has a more pleasing ring: three self-contained groups of figures, from the eighteenth, nineteenth and twentieth centuries respectively, hinged together in a continuing comedy of terrors.

The ancestral wraiths at my own elbow are (amongst other things) Scots-Irish, Northern English, immigrant Huguenot . . . in short the usual Belfast mongrel crew, who have contrived between them to entangle me in the whole Irish-British cat's cradle and thus to bequeath to me a subject for drama which is comprised of multiplying dualities: two islands (the 'British Isles'), two Irelands, two Ulsters, two men fighting over a field.

II

Plays and ghosts have a lot in common. The energy which flows from some intense moment of conflict in a particular time and place seems to activate them both. Plays intend to achieve resolution, however, whilst ghosts appear to be stuck fast in the quest for vengeance. Ghosts are uncompleted souls; witness the Phantom Bride in *Northern Star*, handing on to the Phantom Fiddler in *Heavenly Bodies*, and he in turn to *Pentecost*'s Lily Matthews – in whom the cycle of retribution is in

fact finally laid to rest, in the only way I can foresee as
having any possible meaning.

III

So far as the 'real' characters are concerned, they have
been drawn from the marginalia of the historical record
rather than its main plot. Henry Joy McCracken was a
minor figure in the '98 Rising in Ireland; not enough is
known about him. Dion Boucicault was unarguably a
major force in the Victorian theatre, but then that is a
period of drama which is in itself considered marginal
nowadays; rather more than enough is known about
him. McCracken's mistress, Mary Bodle, is so obscure
that her name might well have been Boall. Boucicault's
Mephistosphelean sparring partner, Johnny Patterson,
survives precariously as a name on fading sheet-music
covers. He certainly did write 'The Garden Where the
Praties Grow', as well as 'The Hat My Father Wore'
(which, suitably altered, was to be taken over as the
favourite anthem of Orangeism) . . . and also,
incidentally, 'The Stone Outside Dan Murphy's Door', a
record of which was the most cherished offering on my
grandfather Jimmy Lynas's old wind-up gramophone.
Harold Wilson, whose recorded voice is briefly heard in
the third play, was Prime Minister of the United
Kingdom of Great Britain and Northern Ireland in the
years 1964–70 and 1974–76.

IV

The first play employs pastiche as a strategy, and the
second one a kind of collage; the third play is written in
a form of heightened realism. This seemed most
appropriate for my own generation, finally making its
own scruffy way on to the stage of history and from
thence into the future tense, in this climactic piece.

Stewart Parker
1989

Northern Star

Northern Star was first performed at the Lyric Players' Theatre, Belfast, on 7 November 1984 with the following cast:

Henry Joy McCracken	Gerard McSorley
Mary Bodle	Emer Gillespie
Phantom Bride/Belle Martin/ Cecily Hamill	Mary Jackson
Peggy Barclay/Mary-Anne McCracken	Marcella Riordan
Thomas Russell/Second Orangeman/Sergeant of Dragoons/ Gorman/Shanaghan	John Hewitt
Samuel Neilson/Captain of Dragoons/Teeling	Liam O'Callaghan
Jimmy Hope	Louis Rolston
Patrick Hamill/Wolfe Tone/ McFadden/Warden/ Interrogator	Paddy Scully
Girvan/Bunting/Haslett	Mark Mulholland

Directed by Peter Farago
Designed by Joe Vanek
Lighting by Trevor Dawson

Act One

Ireland, the continuous past. A farm labourer's cottage on the slopes of the Cavehill outside Belfast. The dark ridge of the hill looms up in the background, silhouetted against the cloudy night sky. Behind the clouds is a paper moon. The cottage is a semi-ruin, half-built and half-derelict. There is a loft and a downstairs room. The sloping roof is partly thatched over, but most of the rafters are fully exposed: those to stage left are raw and unfinished, whilst the stage right ones are charred and twisted. The end walls of the house offer a similar contrast: the stage right gable is a jagged, crumbling ruin, whilst the stage left one is half-built, with neatly stepped stones.

We are looking at the cottage interior as though from the exposed rear aspect. The loft floor extends towards us for only about half the depth of the building with crude wooden stairs as its centre edge, leading down into the main room. There is a bed on one side of the loft, and a child's crib on the other. A length of rope is coiled round the massive main roof beam, just above the stair well. At ground level there is, upstage, the interior front wall of the cottage, with the door centre and small windows on either side. The fireplace is in the stage right gable, and a box bed, curtained over, in the stage left one. The furniture is sparse and battered – kitchen table and chairs, a sideboard, shelves with jugs and tankards.

The entire structure occupies virtually all of the stage's height and width; but it stops short of the whole depth. There is a shallow forestage area outside of its confines. A lambeg drum and a bodhran are placed down left on this forestage. These drums are played by members of the company, who may each play several roles in the action. A change of role may be accomplished merely by a change of hat, coat or wig, in a style which reflects the deliberate anachronisms and historical shifts of the successive scenes. Darkness.

Mary Bodle *quietly crooning a lullaby.*

Mary (*singing*)
   I have seen a lark over high Ardmore,
   Heard his song up in the blue –
   I've heard the blackbird pipe his notes,
   The thrush and the linnet too. . .

The moon comes out. In its spectral light, **Mary Bodle** *can be seen by the crib, gently rocking it, and* **Henry Joy McCracken** *can be seen lying on the bed, dressed only in his britches.*

Mary (*singing*)
   . . . but there's none of them can sing so sweet,
   My singing bird, as you,
   Ah-ah-ah ah-ah
   Ah-ah-ah ah-ah
   My singing bird, as you. . .

McCracken *lights a candle by the bed. He carries it across to examine the rope coiled on the beam.*

Mary (*singing*)
   . . . If I could lure my singing bird
   From his own cosy nest,
   If I could catch my singing bird,
   I would warm him on my breast –
   For there's none of them can sing so sweet,
   My singing bird, as you. . .

McCracken *sets the candle on the ground. He ties a noose on the frayed end of the rope dangling from the beam.* **Mary** *continues to sing quietly, as he speaks.*

McCracken   'Twas the night before Harry was stretched. And the boys they all paid him a visit. (*Stepping forward.*) Citizens of Belfast, the story so far. I stand here before you on the gallows tree, condemned to die for your sake. I stand guilty of nurturing a brotherhood of affection between the Catholics of this town and my fellow Protestants. I stand guilty of cherishing the future happiness of our country above that of my insignificant self. I go willingly to my death

in the true faith of a Presbyterian, confident in the blind
belief that you will all unite together in freedom this
week next week sometime never and I hope you folk at
the back can hear me, then and not till then let my
autograph be given, R.I.P., no flowers at the house
please, notice the rope, by the way, best quality sisal,
sixpence the yard, from my father's own ropeworks,
orders to be taken immediately following the execution,
thanks for nothing.

Mary (*she has stopped singing*)   Quit it, Harry.

McCracken   It's the famous last words, you can see I
need the practice. Imagine standing there mumbling,
Would you mind if I just glanced over my notes, I
won't be a minute.

Mary   So you actually *want* to be hung, is that it?

McCracken   Why, do you think they offer you a
range of alternatives – a brand new eiderdown, or a
holiday for two in the Isle of Man?

Mary   Well, just you practise away at the brave crack,
I'm away to bed.

McCracken   Is the child asleep yet?

Mary   She's dead to the world.

McCracken (*moving across, looking into the crib*)   Dead to
the world is right. What I wouldn't give to sleep like
that . . .

Mary   You're still a free man. They haven't caught
you.

McCracken   Not quite yet.

Mary   You've a whole new life ahead of you. Come
on to bed, Harry.

McCracken   It's a gag to think of this place as a safe
house, isn't it? (*Shaking a loose timber.*) We're in more

danger from the masonry here than we are from the yeomanry, one good belch would bring it down round our ears. I should never have eaten those peas.

Mary Very funny, if it wasn't for the fact that you never touched your supper.

McCracken How did it get like this, was it burnt out? It doesn't even look fully built.

Mary It's not. My cousin O'Keefe was building away at it for himself and his bride-to-be. She came up one morning and found him lying dead – on the floor down there – and the place half-destroyed. The people blamed it on the stones.

McCracken Stones?

Mary He'd took stones from the fairy fort on the hill up there, for the building.

McCracken Oh, I'm with you, the revenge of the little people. Another triumph for the Age of Reason.

Mary He was a freethinker, O'Keefe. People hated him.

McCracken Did they now? In that case we can eliminate the fairy folk from the inquiry, I'd say. What happened to the bride-to-be?

Mary It put her astray. She come up here on the wedding night, in her dress and veil, and hung herself from that rope you've been playing the fool with.

McCracken *revises his attitude to the rope.*

McCracken So. The old refrain. Every joke turning into a nightmare. Every nightmare into a joke. That's an Irish lullaby.

Mary She's often seen waiting by the door out there. They say any man that looks her straight in the eye is a dead man. Which is why it's a safe house.

McCracken   Protected by the Phantom Bride. So be it. For one last night. That's very quaint. A quaint way to go for the man of Reason.

Mary   Will you quit that wild nonsense, once and for all, you know your sister's coming with documents, by this time tomorrow you could be on the seas to America.

McCracken   They have their exits and their entrances and one man in his time plays many parts, his acts being seven ages. Or in my case, seven years. That's all it's been.

Mary   Some seven years.

McCracken   You've no notion of what it was all about, have you?

Mary   I'm a gamekeeper's daughter, with a bastard child to rear, I've no head on me for all your dreams of glory.

McCracken   There was a new idea, Mary. We thought we were its midwives. What did it mean to be Irish? When you distilled it right down to the raw spirit? It meant to be dispossessed, to live on ground that isn't ours, Protestant, Catholic, Dissenter, the whole motley crew of us, planted together in this soil to which we've no proper title. . .

Mary   I've got no wit for this, Harry.

McCracken   Listen to me! Please. Just this night. Look at me. My great-grandfather Joy was a French Huguenot, my great-grandfather McCracken was a Scottish Covenanter, persecuted, the pair of them, driven here from the shores of home, their home but not my home, because I'm Henry Joy McCracken and here to stay, a natural son of Belfast, as Irish a bastard as all the other incomers, blown into this port by the storm of history, Gaelic or Danish or Anglo-Norman, without distinction, it makes no odds, every mother's son of us children of nature on this sodden glorious patch of earth, unpossessed of deed or inheritance, without distinction, for the only distinction that matters is between the power and the wealth on the one hand and the bent knee on the other, and we all of us suffer the bent knee, every one, and for why? Because the power isn't ours and the wealth isn't ours, they ebb and they flow from another source, always and only the one source, the island of hope and glory across the water . . .

Mary   They let you have your parliament, but that wasn't good enough.

McCracken   One can't let the animals run the zoo. One appoints keepers. Gentlemen of rank and fortune. Chaps like one that one can trust to keep the cages bolted and barred. That was the parliament they let us have. The zoological theory of government. But we preferred the logical one. Irish animals unite. Unite! Let the natural sons come into their inheritance. Catholic Protestant Dissenter, one big mongrel family, that was it. The new idea. And we were meant as its midwives. . . except that we botched the birth, you see, arse over tip, up to our oxters in bright red blood, the misshapen foetus scrabbing feebly away at the face of death, and the mother howling her entrails out, with the ring of logical faces round her, all concerned, all at a loss, mine amongst them, Henry Joy McCracken, fanfare please, Commander-in-Chief of the United Irish Army of the North, brave croppy boys who fear no noise on the green hills of Holy Ireland and we couldn't even capture Antrim, have you ever been to Antrim, I mean it isn't exactly Paris, is it, it's scarcely Boston, it's not quite Philadelphia, is it?

Mary *grabs him by the shoulders and shakes him violently.*

Mary   Stop this, stop it, will you just leave it alone?

McCracken   Sure, what's the harm in letting me talk,

it's only talk, harmless words. I'm stripped bare of all the rest. All the great performances. The exits and the entrances, it's history now, the seven ages of Harry. I'm down to the bare, harmless words, nothing more. A bit of brave crack. A positively last appearance.

Mary God, to think of all the times when I could scarcely get a word out of you. Into bed without so much as hello-there. (*He remains lost in thought.*) Come on to bed now, love.

McCracken We botched the birth, Mary. The womb may never come right again. Christ knows what hideous offspring it may bring forth from this day on.

Mary You know, you should go on the stage, you.

McCracken Haven't we always been on a stage, in our own eyes? Playing to the gods. History, posterity. A rough, hard audience. Thundering out our appointed parts, the Mudlers' Club, God help us. A bunch of wet-lipped young buckos, plotting how to transform the world from Peggy Barclay's back room. Ballads and toasts, toasts and ballads. Speechifying. Pub talk. Declarations and Resolutions of this, that and the other, I'd no patience with it all, I wanted to be up and doing.

Mary Don't I know it.

McCracken Neilson pontificating away at the head of the table, Tommy Russell rhapsodising into his enth pint, Jimmy Hope banging on about his labouring classes. . .

As he speaks, the ghostly figures of **Neilson, Russell** *and* **Hope** *glide into the downstairs room and assume the positions he is describing.*

McCracken And where did it all go at the end of the evening? Pissed away into the gutter, flowing away into the night. That was the Mudlers' Club for you, better named than we knew then. The Age of Innocence, that was.

Mary   Sure you used to imitate them all for me.

McCracken   Oh, aye. I could always be relied upon for the funny voices. (*In* **Russell***'s voice.*) 'This Year of Our Lord 1791'. . .

Neilson *and* **Hope**   Saint Patrick's night!

Russell   Gentlemen, pray arm yourselves.

He hands out tankards to **Neilson** *and* **Hope***, and pours beer from a jug for them and himself.* **McCracken** *meanwhile leads* **Mary** *to the bed with the candle, then blows it out.*

McCracken   One short night. Why does it have to be in July? Why could it not be a nice long night in December?

Mary   We'd be foundered if it was.

McCracken   We just have to try and lift it altogether out of time!

He lifts her in his arms. The bodhran plays softly.
McCracken *lowers* **Mary** *into the bed, gets in beside her. The moon goes behind a cloud. Darkness.*

McCracken   No future. No past. Just you and me. This night, Mary. Out of time.

The bodhran plays more urgently. The figure of the **Phantom Bride** *appears at a downstairs window, peering in. The figures of* **Neilson**, **Russell** *and* **Hope** *within are caught motionless in her special light, holding aloft their tankards.* **Russell** *suddenly raps the table with a gavel. The bodhran stops. The* **Phantom Bride** *disappears.*

Russell, **Neilson** and **Hope**   Health to the Mudlers!

Lights come up on them as they salute with their tankards a large wooden signboard above the mantelpiece which reads 'Mudlers' Club'.

Russell (*with another rap of the gavel*)   Begin!

They commence a race to drain their tankards dry. From the downstage shadows, the tavern keeper **Peggy Barclay** *emerges on to the forestage and addresses the house.*

Peggy   Such a night for noise and villainy! An honest man mayn't trust in his own shadows, i'faith, that he may not. Nay, nor even in his very dreams, lest he mumble aught in his sleep, for as the saying is – walls have ears to hear. Never was honest innkeeper put upon as I am! A frolic of young bucks carousing nightly in my tavern, boasting freely of how they will turn out Grattan's Parliament and plant a true democracy in the land. And all the while a spying eye at every keyhole. Still they brag, howso'er I upbraid them for't. There's falsehood in fellowship, sez I. Charge our glasses, Peggy, sez they. Lackadays, was ever such times as these? But then the Golden Age was never the present one – as the saying is. Howsomever, I have smoked out one particular scheming miss in my own kitchen, in troth I have. Tonight will see her treachery amply rewarded, strike me dead if it don't, the worthless bawd. Old saws speak truth, and truth's a pointed thing – She that steals honey should beware the sting!

She slips back into the shadows, as **Russell**, *finishing his beer first, bangs the empty tankard down on the table.*

Russell   Done!

Hope (*following suit*)   Done!

Neilson (*coming last*)   Undone, the devil take't.

Russell   Last man pays.

Hope   Settle up, honest Samuel.

Neilson   A pox on this thick ale! 'Twere easier supped with a spoon.

Russell   'Tis three parts Lagan mud.

Hope   Much like the brains of her that brewed it, I fear.

Neilson   Hush, she approaches. (*Aside.*) With a proverb at the ready, I doubt not.

Peggy Barclay *enters the room.*

Peggy   Now then, good sirs, I trust you keep well, but then well is that well does, in my estimation.

Neilson   True indeed, Peggy, and you shall do well by us – if you'll fetch us your finest wine.

Peggy   'Faith, Mr Neilson, haven't I a fresh pipe of choice Barcelona, which I did not yet pierce. I have reserved the maidenhead of it for your pleasure.

Neilson   Let it be ravished forthwith. You may lay the deflowering to my account.

Peggy   Presently, but I entreat a word in your ears, good sirs.

Russell (*aside*)   Oh, Lord, she will moralise us into sobriety. (*Rapping with the gavel.*) Mistress Barclay has the floor.

Hope   She has the walls and roof to boot, Thomas.

Peggy   Indeed I do, Mr Hope, and as long as it remain so, you may discourse together as freely as you please. Ale-sellers should not be tale-tellers. But as the saying is – a nudge is as good as a blinker to a dead horse.

Neilson (*aside*)   'Sblood – the proverbs grow as muddy as the ale.

Peggy   Malicious tongues may wag. I can vouch for my own in that regard – but I cannot always vouch for others.

Belle Martin *appears from the bed in the loft, and descends*

*the stairs to the downstairs room, hastily straightening up her
blouse and skirt.*

Peggy   Belle Martin, where have you kept yourself to
this o'clock?

Belle   I have been abed, I have a distemper in the gut.

Neilson   With no shortage of bedfellows to account for
it, I warrant.

Belle   None of this company has had the honour, I
can vouch for that.

Peggy   We'll have no raillery, miss. Fetch more ale for
these gentlemen.

Russell   The wine, Peggy, the wine, I beseech you. . .
(*But* **Belle Martin** *has gone.*)

Peggy   Presently, Mr Russell, presently. What I'm
advising you of is – a tight mouth traps no flies. Prithee
watch your tongues – in your cups – if you catch my
drift.

Neilson   Egad, Peggy, thou'rt a wise woman. This
room is indeed become an academy of scandal. To think
of what McCracken said last night about Lord
Killowen!. . . but I dare not whisper it.

Peggy   Oh, 'tis safe enough with me, Mr Neilson.

Neilson   Why, it seems that his lordship owns negro
slaves, in Virginia. And these same black slaves have
volunteered subscriptions, to a Relief Fund.

Peggy   A Relief Fund? To what end?

Neilson   For the relief of his lordship's Catholic
tenants in Westmeath.

Russell   Nay, Samuel, 'tis a brazen lie. His lordship is
merely shipping the niggers over here.

Peggy   Over to Ireland? To what end, Mr Russell?

Russell   To educate his Catholics in the art of picking cotton.

Peggy   Fie on you, sirs, you predestinate with me. But be warned – for predestination is the thief of time. As the saying truly is.

Belle Martin *re-enters with the ale and starts to serve it.*

Peggy   You know well that rash ideas have been noised about in this room – aye, and reported too. And here's the lass can tell you how! (*Seizing* **Belle Martin** *by the arm.*)

Belle (*struggling*)   Leave be, I've said nothing!

Peggy   I found one of your billet-doux to Sovereign Bristow, madam tittle-tattle!

Belle   Leave be, I say, you oul' she-dragon!

In the struggle, a paper falls from **Belle Martin***'s sleeve.*

Russell (*stooping to pick it up*)   Stay! A purloined paper, if I mistake it not.

Belle   That paper is my business, pray give it over, sir. . . (*Snatching for it.*)

Peggy   Not so hasty, madam spy. Your fancy words won't butter no parsimony, not with me.

Russell   Well, well. Here is fine matter indeed. Pray read it to the company, Belle.

Belle   Read it yourself.

Peggy   Do what you're bid, if you hope to 'scape a whipping.

Belle Martin *sullenly takes the paper and reads from it.*

Belle   'Declaration and Resolution of the Society of United Irishmen of Belfast . . .'

Neilson   'Sblood!

Hope   Pray continue, Belle.

Belle 'First Resolved, that the weight of English influence in the government of this country is so great, as to require a cordial union among all the people of Ireland to maintain that balance which is essential to the preservation of our liberties and the extension of our commerce.'

Neilson Handsomely phrased thus far – if I may say so in all modesty. Although I find the rendition somewhat lacking in spirit. A touch more liveliness, Belle, if you please.

Belle 'Second, that the sole con. . . const . . .'

Russell Constitutional.

Belle . . . 'constitutional mode by which that influence can be opposed, is by a complete and. . . and. . .'

Hope Radical.

Belle . . . 'radical reform of the representation of the people in Parliament.'

Russell (*holding her shoulders, reading over them*) 'Third, that no reform is practicable, efficacious or just, which shall not include Irishmen of every religious persuasion.'

Hope So, Belle Martin, what think you of these sentiments?

Belle The likes of me is not paid to think but to serve.

Peggy You've been serving two masters, hussy, but you'll not serve no longer in this house, for I'm serving notice on you, here and now.

Russell Come, Peggy, you deal too harshly. These sentiments are legal – as well as sensible. The wench has served us well by disseminating them round the town.

Neilson Most true, let us furnish her at once with further copies.

Peggy   Alack, sirs, there's more fish than this in the kettle. She has writ down, I warrant ye, the list of all your secret committee.

Hope   Is that the truth, Belle Martin? Where have you this list?

McCracken *has stolen out of bed and donned a shirt. He appears coming down the stairs, buttoning the shirt up, holding a paper.*

McCracken   'Tis well in hand, citizen Hope.

Belle (*aside*)   Confound him, he has but trifled with me!

Neilson   Zounds, Harry, is that her actual paper?

McCracken   Still warm, Samuel – from where it was worn, close to the heart.

Neilson   Pour the fellow a bumper, Peggy, he has outflanked even your intelligence.

Peggy   In troth, Mr McCracken, but you're a canny man, and as the saying is – the brains don't lie in the beard.

Hope   This stratagem should be a story worth the telling.

McCracken   Nay, Jimmy, the tale of an average fellow home from the wars, nothing more.

Neilson   Methinks 'twas an ambuscade of the country sort.

McCracken   What say you, Belle?

Belle   You have used me ill, but your own day will come, and may hell roast the whole crowd of you!

Peggy   Still your insolent tongue, madam. You're going out on the street where you belong this very minute! Bell, book and baggage!

She marches **Belle Martin** *out.*

Russell (*with a bang of the gavel*)   Citizen McCracken, stand forth.

McCracken   Yours to command, citizen chairman.

Russell   Kindly oblige us with a blow-by-blow of this engagement, sir.

McCracken   I own I had first thought of sending in Lieutenant Jimmy Hope here, the drab has always harboured a special fondness for him.

Neilson   'Twould have proved a forlorn Hope, I warrant.

Hope   I plead a wife – fully deployed in arms, on another field.

McCracken   Exemption granted. So, gentlemen, I was obliged myself to launch a single-handed frontal assault.

Russell   It would appear that you soon enough gained the initiative.

McCracken   I attained her breastworks, fired my bastinadoes – and she was quite o'er run.

Neilson   Bravo!

McCracken   With the plunder well stowed, I concluded an equable peace and retired from the field.

Russell (*a bang of the gavel*)   Citizen Mudlers, I give you Mr McCracken's famous victory!

They drink the toast, and grimace at the ale.

Neilson   Let us trust that you have suffered no lasting injury from the engagement.

McCracken   I can vouchsafe this, Samuel. If I have caught the clap, then in that respect at least Lord Castlereagh and I are brothers-in-arms.

Russell   My thunder . . . Belle Martin . . . she is become his lordship's whore?

McCracken   He is even now preparing Dublin apartments for her accommodation. I smoked out the very street.

Hope   And this the cur that we fought to get elected, the people's supposed champion, the apostle of reform – who now sets his whore to spy on us!

Russell   A dog in office, without question.

Neilson   So much for the moderate man.

Hope   There is a tyranny in such moderation.

Russell   A pox on all moderation! Send round that ale.

McCracken   Gladly.

Neilson   Castlereagh – 'sblood! The devil take him, and his confounded Northern Whig Club! Swilling down his turtle soup, in between regaling us with his fine hollow toasts!

McCracken (*aristocratic voice*)   'Gentlemen – pray drink to our Sovereign Lord – the People!'

Neilson   P'shaw!

McCracken (*as before*)   'Pray drink to President Washington and the United States of America!'

Russell   I could swear 'twas his very voice.

McCracken   'Pray drink success to the Gallic constitution' – (*Own voice.*) so long as it remains safely in France.

Neilson   Enough of that canting Judas. Let us drink good wine to the honest words of Jimmy Hope, from his Volunteer banners. (*Shouting.*) Peggy! (*Speaking.*) How went it, Jimmy?

Hope   'The Irish Bastille – let us unite to destroy it.'

Russell   'Our Gallic brother was born July 14th, 1789

– alas! We are still in embryo!'

Hope   What I contend is – Castlereagh is the
landlords' darling, and Grattan the darling of the
merchants. The men of rank and the men of fortune.
They contend one with another – but for nothing more
than the people's soul, citizens. They may modify
abuses, they may enact humane and liberal laws. But
they will join forces to cut the tongue from anyone who
seeks the freedom of the likes of me – a common
weaver. The swinish multitude is what we are to them.

Neilson   They cannot contend for ever against half a
million Protestant Dissenters, and three million Catholics,
Jimmy.

Russell   If the twain but once unite.

Neilson   They shall unite. It is we who shall unite
them. Let you weave their raiment, Jimmy, whilst I print
their hopes and dreams. Russell's library will educate
'em. And as for McCracken here – he shall woo them
into the one bed.

McCracken   Give us a song, Jimmy, before we grow
entirely pious.

Russell   Sing us your ditty about Moral Force, pray.

McCracken   'Sdeath, not a pious song, in pity's name.

Neilson   'Tis a good lusty fighting song, sing away,
Jimmy.

Hope (*sings*)
     I see an army
     Of phantom soldiers
     From servile bondage
     They seek recourse
     They bear no muskets
     They fire no cannon
     They fly the colours
     Of Moral Force.

Music. The other three rise and join in.

Hope, Neilson, Russell and **McCracken** (*singing*)
We wear no scarlet
We sound no trumpet
Yet we are warriors
Of great resource
We know the outcome
We march in triumph
We are the Army
Of Moral Force. . .

Neilson, Russell *and* **Hope** *move off.* **McCracken** *seats himself half-way up the stairs. The music comes to an end.*

McCracken   Night before Harry was stretched. Boys they all paid him a visit. . .

Mary (*stirring in bed*)   Harry . . . ?

McCracken   Moral Force. Couldn't miss. We had it taped. All of seven ages ago. Seven ages of Harry. That was the first age, you see. Childhood. The Age of Innocence.

Mary   Harry, where are you? (*Getting out of bed.*) Are you all right, did you have a dream?

McCracken   I did have a dream, days ago, the last time I slept, it was, yes. I was walking alone into town in the broad moonlight, you see, the streets bright as day and deserted except for a roan stallion astray its hooves echoing off the silent walls like gunfire . . . down past our house in Rosemary Lane to Bridge Street. This week they've hung two of my men from Antrim. . . James Dickey the Crumlin lawyer and John Storey the printer of the *Northern Star*, along with two of the Ballynahinch men . . . the heads have all been hacked off and impaled on spikes up on the Market House. I turned up High Street led by the stallion. The four severed heads were staring down at me as I approached, the eyes bulging out the hair stirring in the wind. I

stood in the middle of High Street in the broad
moonlight transfixed by their gaze my own eyes
wouldn't close I felt tears on my face I brushed them
away they were blood-red the heads slowly started to
laugh they laughed and laughed and then the laugh
turned into a howl I covered my ears but the howling
was from my own head . . .

Mary (*coming to him*)   A nightmare, love, that's all it
was!

McCracken   A nightmare, sure enough. It'll turn into
a joke soon.

Mary   A strong punch is what you need. You've got to
get some sleep, Harry.

McCracken   No sleep, not before time. There's six
more ages to straighten out. That's first. I'll be sleeping
for long enough soon.

Mary   No more of that talk, I won't have it!

McCracken   I led an army of men into a charnel
house the other week, so what'll it be, the price of
bread, the shocking weather we've been having?

Mary   With or without you they would have marched,
to exactly the same tune. It's done with. You've a life to
live.

McCracken   There was a man joined us just this
morning, on the far side of the hill, Mary. He went
through Antrim after the battle was over. He saw a
dead-cart piled high with bodies, it was halted by a
yeomanry captain. The captain asked the burial party,
where the devil did these vermin come from? One of
the mangled corpses on the cart raises his head and
says, 'I come frae Ballyboley'. Nightmare turns to joke.
They all roared themselves silly. Then they buried him
along with the rest.

Mary   So you thought they'd kiss and make up?

McCracken   What do I know about soldiering? A moonstruck linen merchant. All I saw was my own life, as a forfeit, willingly offered.

Mary   Well, you were let off, free of charge. A gift from God, you should cherish it.

McCracken   One last night with you, Mary. That's the gift I cherish.

Mary   One night won't do. You're not yet thirty-one years old, our Lord himself did better than that. You've been four weeks on the run, you're done in and you need your sleep. I'm away to my da's house to mix you a draught.

McCracken   Leave it, Mary, in God's name, don't squander the time. It's not sleep I want. It's your thighs round me.

Mary   I won't fornicate with a ghost – with a man on a dead-cart. The country's full enough of them, I want the man I loved, Harry. The man who gave me that child. You'll have the means of your own deliverance, as soon as your sister comes. For the time being you need your sleep. (*Putting on a shawl.*) I'm away to fetch the punch. (*Going to the front door.*) Keep an eye on her, I won't be long.

She exits through the door. **McCracken** *stands by the crib.*

McCracken   So what do you think, Maria? What do you make of your fathead of a da? A long shadow in the moonlight... that's about it for you... except you'll have to live your life in that shadow, God love you, Harry's little indiscretion, as opposed to all his big ones... like his quaint notion of roaming round the countryside, hell bent on uniting together the Prods and the Papes. On account of how they were slaughtering each other in gangs, you see. The Peep O'Day Boys versus the gallant Defenders. (*Moving to head of stairs.*) Harry Steps In. A popular melodrama. Scene – the county of Armagh. Nature has lavished its bounty. But civil strife rends asunder the peaceful rustic Eden. Enter the noble and fearless young McCracken – uniting the rabble in a common love for his shining youthful ardour. Music, please.

Melodrama music from off. **McCracken** *descends the stairs.* **Patrick Hamill**, *clutching a sheaf of papers, steals on to the forestage.*

Hamill   Hist! Who comes hence to my humble cabin with such despatch? Is it friend or foe?

McCracken   Peace, good fellow. I am Henry Joy McCracken, come to assist as best I may in your hour of tribulation.

Hamill   May heaven smile upon your honour!

McCracken   You are Patrick Hamill of Loughgall?

Hamill   That I am, sir, and you're more than welcome to my humble abode, for all the brave work you've been doing on our poor account.

Music stops.

McCracken   What papers have you there, Patrick? Have you the deposition you made to Mr Grier, the magistrate?

Hamill   That I have indeed, sir, bless you. He enquired first if I was of the Popish faith and I answered yes, 'Well then,' sez he, 'you are well known in this district to be croppy renegades, and you will pay the price on this circuit at any rate, case dismissed.'

McCracken (*aside*)   Infamous scoundrel. (*To* **Hamill**.) So the mutilation of your livestock and the insults offered to your wife, these were not even admitted by him as evidence?

Hamill   Bless you, sir, that they were not.

McCracken   Patrick, a word with you. Mr Cuthbert and I are engaged in contesting such cases as yours. We mean to apply the law against those blackguards who administer it unjustly.

Hamill   An may God reward you for it, sir. D'ye know, I have a cousin wrought for your sister, in the town of Belfast, at the weaving, and she had the highest regard for all your connection.

McCracken   Indeed, my sister Mary-Anne is universally beloved. Now then, show me your papers. (*Taking them.*) Before we can proceed in a case, we have to be certain sure that all that was told unto us is the whole truth of the matter.

Hamill   That you do, sir, indeed.

McCracken (*leafing through the papers*)   What's this?

Hamill   Oh, that was posted on the door there, just yesterday night.

McCracken (*reading*)   'Go to Hell – Connaught Wouldn't Have You – Fire and Faggot!' Did the Peep O'Day boys do this?

Hamill   Saving your grace, it's no longer the Peep O'Day Boys they call themselves in this townland. As I hear it.

McCracken   What, then?

Hamill   Why, the Orange Boys. (*Music.*)

McCracken   Attend me, Patrick – did you ever hear tell of the Society of United Irishmen?

Hamill   D'ye know, I recall Mr Cuthbert mentioning something of the sort, when he was dacent enough to trouble himself with our wee bit of bother.

McCracken   Mr Cuthbert and I are officers in the Society. We abide by a simple creed – there is strength

in union, weakness in dissension. It is not the Peep
O'Day Boys or the Orange Boys who threaten your
livelihood and life. They themselves are your fellow
prisoners, in this vast cage that we call a country. It is
the landlords and the magistrates – the Mr Griers of this
county – the gentlemen of rank and fortune, who
deliberately foment this kind of rancour between you
and your neighbours, for their own greater security.
They are the cruel jailers we must unite to oppose! Do
you comprehend me?

Hamill   Say no more, Mr McCracken, for I'm your
man, and plenty like me, whenever you care to say the
word.

Music stops. **Cecily Hamill** *comes rushing in through the door.*

Cecily   Fly, Pat, fly in heaven's name, they're a-
coming for to murder us!

Hamill   Merciful providence! Are they close yet?

Cecily   They're in the loanen!

Hamill (*bolting the door*)   Mr McCracken, begone, sir,
begone! They'll not offer you any insult.

McCracken   Who is it that approaches, Mrs Hamill?

Cecily   'Tis the Orange Boys!

*Two men in orange sashes and with scarves round their faces have
passed the outside of the window.* **Hamill** *fetches a pike from the
inside of the chimney breast. Thundering on the door.*

Girvan (*from outside door*)   Come out of that, you Papist
rebel, or we'll fire the house round you!

McCracken   I have a mind to talk with these
gentlemen, kindly put up your pike.

Hamill   Divil the talk you'll get from them, it's blood
alone they're after.

McCracken *moves to the door.*

Cecily   In God's name, sir, don't be letting them in on us!

McCracken   Restrain your fear, good woman. No harm will befall you, on my honour.

She falls on her hands and knees, saying her rosary.
McCracken *unbolts the door and opens it. The two*
Orangemen *confront him, holding a scythe and a billhook.*

McCracken   I wish you good morning, gentlemen. And whom do we have the pleasure of addressing?

Girvan   Thrustout and Thrasham, that's the only names you'll be needing to know.

McCracken   Mr Hamill is engaged with me on a legal matter, I feel sure he would be happy to accommodate you at a more convenient time.

Second Orangeman   Let him answer to us now, and his girn of a wife along with him.

They push past **McCracken** *into the room, the latter turns on his heel and plucks the scarf from the face of the* **First**
Orangeman*, who rounds upon him, with scythe upraised.*
McCracken *forestalls the blow with a firm grip on the raised arm and gazes into* **Girvan***'s face.*

McCracken   I prefer to talk to a man's face than to his noserag. And here is a face I believe I know. Mr Girvan, is it not, of Richill? I enrolled you as a United man but a month since, Mr Girvan.

He releases his grip, **Girvan** *lowers his scythe.*

Girvan   What odds if you did delude me for a wheen o'days? With all your high-flown blether about tithes and rents and the United cause? There's damn-all call for your Belfast prating and preaching round this parish.

McCracken   If you have grievances to air, then out with them. Mr Hamill is as ready to hear them as I am,

I daresay. (*To* **Second Orangeman**.) You may put up your weapon, friend.

Girvan (*of* **Hamill**)   This man is a sworn leader of the Defenders in this county.

Hamill   And it pleases your grace, 'tis a confounded lie!

Girvan   The attack on Protestants, at the Diamond, a week gone last Thursday, was his doing.

Hamill   Wasn't I winning hay with Shan Durkin on the very day at issue, and the same man will vouch for it?

Second Orangeman   Durkin was seen at the Diamond alongside you.

McCracken   Pray, what befell at the Diamond, Mr Girvan?

Girvan   Damnable treachery, that's what. We were met together peaceably and they thought to catch us out with an ambush, but we were too cute for that.

Second Orangeman   One good skite from us, and they ran for dear life.

Girvan   Not before a good thirty of them were despatched to hell for their pains.

McCracken   Thirty Catholics dead, you say?

Girvan   If not more.

McCracken   I see. And so how many parliamentary votes did you gain? How much land? How many remissions of tithes to your vicar or rents to your landlord? In short – how much power and how much freedom was obtained by these thirty-odd deaths and this glorious and immortal victory?

Girvan   I'll tell you what was gained – the Orange Society. We're organised now, to guard our land and religion and rights against Defender savages the likes of him.

McCracken   Look in the face of this man, who is your neighbour, and tell me truly whether it be the face of a savage, as you say.

Girvan   Go forth and ask Alexander Barclay of Richill the same question. Him and his wife and his thirteen-year-old had their tongues torn out by Defenders, and the wife's body further abused till she died within days of her mutilations. Hamill here can acquaint you further with the details of the case.

Hamill   'Twas no doing of mine or of my connection, as God is my judge.

McCracken   You have magistrates, entirely in your sympathy, to deal with such matters, You cannot pretend that you are defenceless before the law, which certainly is the case with Mr Hamill and his kind.

Girvan   Why must your type always side with the accursed Papist? You're a Presbyterian same as me and him, where's your loyalty?

McCracken   My loyalty is here, Mr Girvan, in this room – but to all of you within it. (*Music.*) The country round here is as lush and lovely as a garden, is it not?

Girvan   What of it?

McCracken   It has riches and rewards a-plenty – more than enough for all like yourselves who labour in it. Tell me, why do you not partake freely of them?

Hamill   Sure, they're not ours to command, Mr McCracken.

McCracken   Ah. But they could and would be, Patrick – if you but cease to rent each other, like caged animals, and join with us, in the true struggle, for our mutual freedom. You know very well there are government agents at large, working to foment these

feuds between you. Be not deluded by them! Every blow
you strike is a self-inflicted wound. Go to your home
now, Mr Girvan, and you, sir, I shall investigate the
affair at the Diamond and report the truth of it to the
authorities.

Music stops. Pause.

Girvan   We may go this time – on your warranty –
but we mean to be satisfied in full.

McCracken   I shall call tomorrow on you both and
take your affidavits. Good-day to you, friends. (*Shaking
hands with them.*) Good-day, sir.

The two **Orangemen** *exit through the door.*

Hamill   May the saints preserve your honour, you
have saved our two lives this day.

Cecily   Indeed you have so, and you'll be forever in
our prayers.

McCracken   Patrick, a word with you. Be honest with
me now. Are you in fact a sworn member of
the Defenders?

Hamill   Bless you, sir, but sure all of us are, round
these parts.

Cecily   Come quick, Pat.

Hamill   Forgive us, sir.

As the lambeg is beaten, **Patrick** *and* **Cecily Hamill** *exit.*
McCracken *ascends the stairs, pauses by the rope. Drum stops.*

McCracken   So much for the second age. Idealism,
they call that. Also known as adolescence. Harry Steps
In, and acts his heart out. Citizens of Belfast – you
rehearse all of your chosen parts and you play them
with the utmost zeal – except that maybe they're really
playing you. Think about it. They costume themselves in
your flesh and bones, borrow your voice, strike your

poses, and at the end they move on – (*Clutching the rope.*) and this is where they leave you hanging.

Mary Bodle *comes in through the front door followed by* **Mary-Anne McCracken**, *who carries two bundles.*

Mary   He's maybe dozed off upstairs.

Mary-Anne   We won't waken him, if he has. I'd rather wait.

McCracken   Mary-Anne, is that you? (*Running down the stairs.*)

Mary-Anne   Harry! (*Embracing him.*) Thank God you're safe.

McCracken   It's you I was worried for, I felt sure you'd been lifted on the road.

Mary-Anne   I've been at Mr Bodle's house since early evening. I didn't dare come on up here until now, the whole of the Cavehill is crawling with militia. (*Putting bundles on table.*)

McCracken   Sit down by the fire, there's still some heat in the embers.

Mary   I'll put this punch by it to keep warm. (*Setting jug of punch in the fireplace.*)

Mary-Anne (*giving her money*)   Mary, this is for you.

Mary   Oh no, Miss McCracken, there's no call for that. . .

Mary-Anne (*forcing it into her hand*)   Not another word. (*To* **McCracken**.) This is a very brave girl, Harry. Venturing out here with me at this hour of the night. . . (*To* **Mary**.) You better run on home now, dear, before your father gets concerned about you. (*Awkward pause.*)

McCracken   In actual fact. . . Mary has been sort of looking out for me.

Mary-Anne   She has indeed, and so has her whole family.

McCracken   She's been staying here, you see. (*Pause.*)

Mary-Anne   Oh, right. Yes. Well. In that case.

Mary   I'll be in the loft, Miss McCracken. Give us a shout if there's anything you need.

Mary-Anne   Thank you, Mary.

Mary *ascends the stairs to the loft and stretches out on the bed.*

McCracken   I'm well cared for.

Mary-Anne   I can see you are.

McCracken   Although the accommodation is a trifle over-ventilated.

Mary-Anne   It's no fit dwelling for a patriot and a hero, that's for certain.

McCracken   Do you mind? You're talking about a charming rural hideaway. Convenient to town. In a much sought-after area.

Mary-Anne   I knew your spirit wouldn't be broken, they all said you'd be in despair, but I told them . . .

McCracken   Any word of Frank and William?

Mary-Anne   Oh, they're both safe hid, they'll be fine.

McCracken   So what about your mother and father and Margaret and John? Not forgetting the bold Atty Bunting?

Mary-Anne   They're all perfectly well, at home. Except that none of us will sleep easy until you're aboard ship and well away, I've brought all the necessaries . . .

McCracken   Come on, I want to hear all the crack about them.

Mary-Anne   They may not understand the struggle as fully as I do, Harry – all the same, you're more than just a beloved son and brother to them now. They cherish and revere you as a national hero, believe me.

McCracken   Fancy a glass of punch?

Mary-Anne   Not one of them would have had you act differently – not even Mother, though she could never bring herself to admit it. Oh, she sent you this, by the way. (*Taking a book from one of the bundles.*) It's Edward Young's *Night Thoughts*, I'm afraid. 'Procrastination is the thief of time' and all that.

McCracken   Her favourite book.

Mary-Anne   Ten thousand lines of sanctimonious gush. Spiritual consolation, she calls it. I told her you'd no need of any such nonsense. What's the loss of one battle in the great war for this country's soul? The coming generations will finish what you've started, they'll model themselves on your example. . .

McCracken   Christ forbid, what an example! Pious phrasemaking over a butcher's shambles, valiant defeat, maudlin self-pity – 'We wuz robbed!' – defeat! What an example. A septic wound. Let them purge the poison and bury us in lime.

Pause.

Mary-Anne   You know that won't be history's verdict. . .

McCracken   History's a whore. She rides the winners.

Pause.

Mary-Anne   You're worn out. Harry. Once you're safe away, you'll be yourself again.

McCracken (*gesturing at the bundles*)   So who am I meant to be in the meantime?

Mary-Anne Oh, yes. . . I had your papers made out
in the name of Owen Pollock, Master Carpenter.
(*Removing them from bundle*.) This is all carpenter's gear and
tools. What you have to do tomorrow, is make your way
to Greencastle, and ask at the quay for a boatman
called Brownlow. He'll take you across to the brig the
Benjamin Franklin, anchored in the Pool of Garmoyle. It's
commanded by a Captain Moore, who's an old
shipmate of father's. Ready?

McCracken Right.

Mary-Anne Name?

McCracken Pollock. Owen Pollock.

Mary-Anne Occupation?

McCracken Carpenter.

Mary-Anne Occupation?

McCracken *Master* carpenter.

Mary-Anne The boatman?

McCracken Brownlow. The Pool of Garmoyle. The
Benjamin Franklin. Captain Moore. Philadelphia, here I
come.

Mary-Anne Well done.

McCracken If only *you* had led the Rising, we would
have walked it.

Mary-Anne Don't poke fun at me, Harry.

McCracken I was never more serious. How have you
been anyway, Mary-Anne?

Mary-Anne Oh, you know. Sit at home. Mind the
business. That's all that's allowed me, I can do nothing,
there's nothing at all I can make happen.

McCracken (*gesturing at bundles*) What do you call this?

Mary-Anne   Did you hear any accounts of the battle at Ballynahinch?

McCracken   I heard the result. That was enough.

Mary-Anne   They found the body of a young girl on the battlefield. Her brother and her lover were comrades-in-arms, on the rebel side. She couldn't bear the thought of losing them both. So she upped and fought alongside them. When the retreat came, the girl couldn't keep up with her two men. So they insisted on staying behind with her... all three were slaughtered, of course. Highly romantic. There were two other female corpses found, standard bearers. Dolled up in green satin as the Goddess of Liberty and the Goddess of Reason. They turned out to be the town whores.

McCracken   That'll please the government.

Mary-Anne   So when the big issues come to be decided, you see, we get cast in the same old roles again. Mothers, wives and mistresses. Goddesses, whores and sisters. Trophies and symbols. The Shan Van Vocht and Roisin Dubh. I presume you love that girl up there?

McCracken   I'm afraid I do.

Mary-Anne (*rising*)   It's time I went.

McCracken   What do you mean? You've scarcely arrived.

Mary-Anne   If I return to David Bodle's house, I can set out for the coast road at first light, and pick up the Belfast coach.

McCracken   You've been the best friend in the world to me, Mary-Anne. From the very beginning.

Mary-Anne   It would ill become me, then, to add to your troubles at this stage.

McCracken   There's nobody I'd sooner have beside me, in a tight corner.

Mary-Anne   As you say – you're well cared for. (*Moving to door.*) I'll not sleep easy till I know that ship has sailed, with you on it.

McCracken   Tell me about Atty Bunting. Is he still collecting away at his folk tunes through all this?

Mary-Anne   You know Atty. Harps on the brain. Harps and organs.

McCracken   Give him my love.

Mary-Anne (*embracing him*)   Oh, Harry!

McCracken   What a sister! Better than I deserve.

Mary-Anne   Don't! We'll talk it all through, in years to come. Not now. Action now, that's what counts. Move carefully.

McCracken   You too.

Mary-Anne   Goodbye.

She leaves quickly through the door.

McCracken (*as she goes*)   Goodbye, Mary-Anne. (*He leans back with a deep sigh of relief against the closed door.*) I have observed . . . that a man is never less true to himself than in the presence of his own family. (*He laughs softly.*) Atty Bunting, his words. The words of the foster son. As touchy as he's clever. With his ancient music of Gaelic Ireland, God love him. Like pins and needles falling into a basin.

Harp music from off. It continues softly right through the following scene.

The Belfast Harp Festival, famous in myth and legend. Forging a national consciousness, we'd got very keen on that by then. A new culture from the old. . . renaissance! That was the third age. The smart talk. The Age of Cleverness.

Atty Bunting *enters from the same side as the sound of the harp music.*

Bunting   May I enquire as to what you are doing
here?

McCracken   I perceive that you are anxious to
explain it to me. By all means do so.

Bunting   Very well. You are standing outside a
musical recital talking to yourself. That is not customary
in polite society. It is a position reserved for beggars and
newspaper critics.

McCracken   My dear Bunting. It is torment enough
to have to listen to the tinkling of your harps – without
the additional penance of gazing upon your harpists.
Until I saw the Irish harpists, I was at a loss as to what
the Irish beggars did with their cast-off clothes.

Bunting   Fortunately, they are not required to return
the compliment – being for the most part blind.
Furthermore, a white waistcoat and a velvet cuff are not
indispensable to good musicianship. However obligatory
they may be to your amateur warmongering.

McCracken   You appear anxious to provoke a quarrel
with me. I do hope it will lead to violence.

Bunting   I abhor violence – apart from that which is
perpetrated by armed men against people whom I
dislike.

McCracken   Do you dislike the whole of Belfast
society, in that case?

Bunting   Only from time to time. On Thursdays they
are tolerable enough. I abominate them on Sunday
afternoons, however. Why do you ask, pray?

McCracken   Twelve harps strung with wire is violence
enough, I venture to suggest. Particularly after two entire
days of listening to them.

Bunting   The preservation of the ancient music of

Ireland is a noble and edifying task. It is profoundly irresponsible of you to expect enjoyment from it.

McCracken   To enjoy the things that are good for us would certainly transform society. It could even be the start of civilised life as we know it.

Wolfe Tone *enters.*

Tone   I perceive that I have interrupted your moralising, gentlemen. I do hope that the damage is irreparable.

McCracken   My dear Tone – no conversation is ever quite complete until you have interrupted it. Are you two gentlemen acquainted?

Bunting   I don't believe I have had the displeasure.

McCracken   Then may I present to you the celebrated Mr Wolfe Tone from Dublin?

Bunting   Tone, did you say? Musical by name, but not, it would seem, by nature.

Tone   I assure you that I esteem the Irish harp above all other instruments – at any rate, up until the point when people begin to pluck at it. I take it I have the honour of addressing the distinguished Mr Edward Bunting?

Bunting   At your service, Mr Tone. May I make bold enough to draw attention to the badge of your society of United Irishmen? It consists of this same harp, bearing the motto – 'It is new strung and shall be heard'. It appears in your case, however, that it shall not in fact be heard after all.

McCracken   That is what vulgar people call hypocrisy. The educated classes refer to it as symbolism.

Tone   You misconstrue our absence from the hall, Mr Bunting. We are conspirators by nature. Conspirators like to listen and hate to be seen. An audience at a musical event has quite the opposite inclination. They go to be seen but never to listen. So you see McCracken and I may prove your truest supporters after all.

Bunting   I am not at all sure that I care for your support. For you the real event of this week is the third anniversary of the Fall of the Bastille. Where the rats released the reptiles from their cages. I speak metaphorically. My metaphor is drawn from zoology.

McCracken   Mr Bunting is of the opinion that the revival of its music will alone suffice to save Ireland. In spite of the worst that his harpists have been able to do.

Tone   Music is the only art above politics. That is why it is the helpless pawn of politics. The old King George adored Handel. I cannot hold that against Handel. It may be the one value held in common between myself and George the Third.

Bunting   Music is only above politics in the way that stars shine above a bog. You would do better, sir, to compare like with like, and say that usury is above politics. Or sodomy perhaps. Or anything else you care to name. For what in the world could be below politics? You will forgive me now, gentlemen, if I return to a better place.

He exits.

Tone   What a very disagreeable fellow, I do hope we shall see more of him. He has quite distracted me from my headache.

McCracken   My dear Tone. You have drunk yourself into a headache on every single night of your visit here. If you had cultivated the loyalist peasantry as vigorously as you have cultivated your headache – why, you might be closer to that uniting of the whole people of Ireland about which you write with such elegance.

Tone   My dear McCracken. I have formulated the

ideology of the entire United movement – galvanised my fellow Protestant radicals in the South – and taken control of the leadership of Catholic opinion. I feel it my duty to leave you and your colleagues up here some trifling work of your own to do.

McCracken   Most considerate, I'm sure. Still, I daresay we may hope to be attended with some little success. . . having originated the entire movement which you subsequently were enlightened enough to join.

Mary Bodle *stirs in the bed.*

Mary   Harry?

Tone   As for my headache – it does not in fact proceed from my trifling consumption of liquor. On the contrary. The consumption of liquor is the only decent cure for it. My headache proceeds from all your confounded Ulster bickering. In this town one feels like a cat let loose in the dog kennels. What with that and Mr Bunting's harpists, I intend to seek a cure this very instant.

He exits.

Mary   Harry? (*She comes to the head of the stairs.*)

McCracken   As to whether the loyalist peasantry is amenable to cultivation. . .

Mary *comes down the stairs to him. The harp music stops.*

Mary   Who were you talking to?

McCracken   What?

Mary   Where's your sister?

McCracken   I was listening to the harp music.

Mary   Harp music? My God, did you think you'd died and gone to heaven or something?

McCracken   He was always great crack, you know.

Mary   Who was?

McCracken   Tone. Him and Russell and Sinclair and
me went down to the docks on that visit, to have a look
over my da's new ship. It was called the *Hibernia* – but
there was a crown painted above the name. He really
took a hand out of me about that.

Mary   Did you drink the punch?

McCracken   I forgot about it.

Mary   Sit down there and I'll pour it for you. (*She does
so.*)

McCracken (*picking up Young's* Night Thoughts)   This is
a better sedative than whiskey. . . 'Procrastination is the
thief of time'. . .

Mary   What are you on about now?

McCracken   It's a poem of over ten thousand lines –
and that's the only one that anybody remembers.
(*Reading.*) 'Fate! Drop the curtain – I can lose no
more. . .' My mother sent it.

Mary   I dozed off, I didn't realise your sister had left.

McCracken   She went back to your da's. Just as well.
I could never have got through the night acting the
patriot hero.

Mary   Does she not know about the child?

McCracken   She didn't even know about you until
tonight.

Mary   She doesn't approve of me much.

McCracken   She has principles. We're a high-minded
sort of family, you see. I had a grandfather, Granda Joy,
– three weeks before he died, at the age of ninety-three,
his leg eaten away with gangrene, he made them carry
him on a dog-cart from Randalstown to Antrim.

Mary   What for?

McCracken   To vote in an election. He was a real
old campaigner, he'd started the *Belfast Newsletter*, he'd
helped to create the Volunteer movement, he'd seen
Grattan's Parliament into office. So there he was, ninety-
three and barely alive, being carried towards the polling
station. My cousin saw him and ran up to him amazed,
and said, 'What brought you here, sir?' The old boy just
glared back at him and barked out, 'The good of my
country!'

Mary   So that's where you get it from.

McCracken   The man he voted into office was
O'Neill, the great moderate reformer. The same John
O'Neill who was killed three weeks ago, in Antrim High
Street – struck through the shoulder blades by one of
my pikemen. That's the sort of family we are all right.
(*He begins to move restlessly about the room*). No surrender on
principles, not an inch. Which is not an untypical
attitude, round these parts. Battling an argument
through to the bitter end. We reached that point in the
Society, soon enough. The Age of Dialectic. Tommy
Russell standing there with his gavel poised. . . (*Banging
the copy of* Night Thoughts *down on the table.*) Begin!

The door is violently burst open and a **Sergeant of
Dragoons** *enters, with blackened face, rifle and bayonet at the
ready.* **Mary** *screams and leaps up.* **McCracken** *stays utterly
calm and composed.*

Sergeant   Nobody move. I'll have the guts of the first
one who moves.

*He briefly checks out the room for other occupants, then returns to
the door and calls through it.*

Only two of them in here, Captain.

A **Captain of Dragoons** *saunters in, face also blackened.*

Captain   Very good, sarnt. The men are searching the

ditches and trees, so you can proceed with the house.

Sergeant Right, sir.

He begins a methodical search of the room.

Captain (*to* **McCracken**) Now, my good man. I require to know your name, and your reasons for being in this picturesque ruin.

McCracken Certainly, Captain. My name is Owen Pollock and I am a master carpenter, employed in the reconstruction of this dwelling.

Captain It is just gone half past two in the morning.

McCracken Is it really? I don't carry a timepiece, you see.

Captain (*picking up documents on the table*) These will be your papers, I expect.

McCracken As you say.

Captain It's deuced accommodating of you to have them so conveniently by.

McCracken I find it advisable in these times always to be prepared to meet the demands of His Majesty's pleasure.

Captain Do you indeed? No doubt with good reason?

McCracken As you say. You see, we are not unaccustomed to sudden visits from His Majesty's servants, in this vicinity.

Captain You have remarkably polished speech for a carpenter.

McCracken Master carpenter.

Captain I beg your pardon.

McCracken I enjoyed the benefits of an enlightened education.

Captain   And where may that have been, pray, the Sorbonne, perhaps?

McCracken   David Manson's school in Belfast. He believed there was a good deal more to learning than the three 'r's.

Captain   I believe that Samuel Neilson and Henry Joy McCracken also ran a school in Belfast, for a spell. They had a novel version of the three 'r's – Reform. Followed by Repression. Followed by Revolution.

McCracken   Join us in a glass of punch, Captain.

Captain   Thank you, I will. Pray do sit down, madam. What, may I ask, is your purpose in being here?

McCracken   This is my wife, Mary.

Captain   I see. Does she normally accompany you on these nocturnal employments? Perhaps she is a master stonemason?

The **Sergeant** *is now ascending the stairs.* **Mary** *stands up again.*

Mary   Wait, Sergeant. (*To* **Captain**.) My child is up there. I should like to be with her while the Sergeant is searching, otherwise she may be frightened.

Captain (*to* **McCracken**)   So you transport your child to the place of work as well, Mr Pollock? This is carrying familial devotion to the point of eccentricity.

Mary   You may as well have the truth, Captain.

McCracken   Mary!

Mary   Why go on with this play-acting? (*To* **Captain**.) I'm not his wife.

Captain   Do pray continue. I have believed nothing so far.

Mary   My name is Mary Bodle. My father is a

gamekeeper. David Bodle, he lives a mile down the road. He doesn't approve of Mr Pollock ... Mr Pollock has been my lover these three years past. The fact is ... you have surprised us in the very act of eloping. We were to be collected from here at midnight by my cousin O'Keefe, who offered to take us to Donaghadee, where we can catch a packet for Scotland tomorrow morning. Something must have happened to delay my cousin, but I know he will come. Fate has thrown us upon your mercy, Captain. You have three innocent lives at your disposal. I beg you to spare us, if only for the child's sake.

Pause.

Captain   I am much affected by your plight, ma'am. I freely confess that I have not been so entertained since the last time I was in the theatre. Sergeant!

Sergeant   Sir.

Captain   Allow Miss Bodle to go ahead of you into the roof space.

Sergeant   Yes, sir.

Mary *goes up the stairs in front of the* **Sergeant***, and stays seated by the crib, while he searches the loft.*

Captain   Your good health, Mr Pollock.

McCracken   And yours, Captain.

Captain   This Mr Bodle perplexes me. Why would he reject such a resourceful fellow as yourself for a son-in-law?

McCracken   You do me an honour, Captain, but the truth of it is – I am a Dissenter, and Mary's family is Catholic.

Captain   They are a desperate breed, these Catholics, are they not?

McCracken   We live in desperate times, do we not?

Captain   They've been slaughtering innocent Protestants down in Wexford, or perhaps you haven't yet heard?

McCracken   You hear so many things.

Captain   Just last month, it was. They put to the torch a barn in Scullabogue, in which they incinerated three hundred Protestant men, women and children. Entire families. In the name of the United Irish nation. Are you a believer in the Irish nation, Mr Pollock?

McCracken   I hope and believe that I'm a patriotic man.

Captain   And what do you expect me to think of that little speech?

McCracken   I never expect a soldier to think, Captain.

Captain (*enjoying himself immensely*)   Nor should you. Nonetheless – I also hope and believe that I'm a patriotic man. Why else would I serve my country? Which country do you think I serve, by the way?

McCracken   You wear the English colours.

Captain   Wrong. Not so. I serve the King, Lords and Commons . . . of Ireland. King George the Third of Ireland and his elected Dublin parliament. As does my company out there in those dark, murderous fields. And every man jack of them is a Catholic peasant from Kerry.

McCracken   A desperate breed. Just as you say.

Captain   Questions of guilt or innocence never detain them overmuch. They like to flog a suspect till they can see his inner organs.

McCracken   Your own position at their head,

Captain, doesn't sound entirely enviable.

Captain I freely own I would much prefer to be in the field against the French. War is bestial, of course. We all agree on that. We still seem to admire the rank and medals which it confers, however. And there are precious few of either to be won in a civil war.

McCracken You consider this a civil war?

Captain The whole history of Ireland is a civil war. It was very comical of these Scotch-Presbyterian drapers and linen merchants to imagine they could make it otherwise. There has never been the least vestige of a nation-state on this island. Nor will be. There have been petty fiefdoms, Gaelic provinces, clan territories, tribal settlements – all of them in a perpetual flux of slander and slaughter. Only one allegiance has ever succeeded in uniting a majority of them – the allegiance to the British crown. Now these United Irishmen have divided them even on that score. It was a dismal farce, was it not? – to behold these high-minded provincial tradesmen – all got up like knights-errant in a stage pageant – leading an alehouse rabble against the professional army of their own countrymen. How could sober citizens the like of those so grotesquely delude themselves, do you suppose – Mr Pollock?

McCracken My enemy's enemy is my friend. Perhaps they believed in that old saying.

Captain You allude to the French. The French were profoundly embarrassed by it all, and greatly relieved that they never did succeed in the attempted invasion.

McCracken You seem remarkably well briefed, Captain.

Captain We had first-rate intelligence at every level of the conspiracy. I see you're a reading man, Mr Pollock.

McCracken A little poetry is good for the soul.

Captain   I expect you know that bookseller in Bridge Street, what the devil's his name?

McCracken   It escapes me too for the moment. Although I have passed his sign often enough.

Captain   John Hughes, is it not? He was a member of the famous Mudlers' Club.

McCracken   The club was well-named, it would appear.

Captain   John Hughes was our man. Right from the beginning. We knew every move that the Belfast Society made. We knew McCracken's plans, for instance, before he had even reached Antrim.

Pause. **McCracken** *smiles.*

McCracken   You'll have him safely locked up by now then, Captain.

The **Sergeant** *comes back down the stairs.*

Sergeant   Nothing to report. Captain.

Captain   Very good, Sergeant. Muster the men.

Sergeant   Yes, sir.

He goes out through the door.

Captain (*rising*)   Now then, Mr Pollock. If you will gather up your possessions, we shall accompany you to the Artillery Barracks.

Pause.

McCracken   Hark ye, Captain – I'd as lief stay where I am, if it's all one to you.

Captain   I'm afraid I have enjoyed our discussion of politics to such a degree, that I feel compelled to continue it, in a less draughty place. Miss Bodle may come too. If you both prove to be the people you say you are, we shall guarantee your safe conduct to

Donaghadee. I own I am not yet entirely beyond the reach of romance.

The **Sergeant** *bursts in again, very flustered.*

Sergeant   Beg pardon, sir.

Captain   What's the matter, Sergeant, you look as though you'd seen a ghost.

Sergeant   God save us, sir, but I have so!

Captain   What the devil do you mean?

Sergeant   If you please, Captain, there's the ghost of a woman standing at the gate.

Captain   Are you mad?

Sergeant   I struck at her with my bayonet and it went clean through.

Captain   You superstitious baboon, get out there and muster the men!

Sergeant   If you please, Captain, the men are away.

Captain   They're what?

Sergeant   The minute they saw her, sir, they took to their heels.

Captain   Get after them, you confounded fool, I'll have you court-martialled for this, come on!

He rushes out through the door, followed by the **Sergeant**. **McCracken** *laughs. From outside the closed door, we hear the* **Captain**'s *death cry. The child in the crib –* **Maria** *– begins to cry.* **McCracken** *goes to the window to look out. Upstairs,* **Mary Bodle** *rocks the crib and begins to sing softly.*

Mary (*singing*)
    It was on the Belfast mountains
    I heard a maid complain,
    And she vexed the sweet June evening

With her heart-broken strain,
Saying woe is me, life's anguish
Is more than I can dree,
Since Henry Joy McCracken
Died on the gallows tree ...

McCracken *moves to centre stage.*

McCracken   Citizens of Belfast ... I never even
bothered taking the Oath till '95. After that, it was in
earnest. Reform, we'd tried for. Repression was what
we'd got. So the desire was hardening, hardening up.
For Revolution.

Mary *(singing)*
... He says, 'My love be cheerful
For tears and fears are vain,'
He says, 'My love be hopeful,
Our land shall rise again,'
He kissed me very fondly,
He kissed me three times o'er,
Saying death shall never part us
My love, for evermore ...

The door swings open. The **Phantom Bride** *stands on the
threshold, bathed in light.*

McCracken *(raising his right hand)*   In the awful presence
of God, I, Henry Joy McCracken, do voluntarily declare
that I will endeavour to forward a brotherhood of
affection, an identity of interests, a communion of rights,
and a union of power, among Irishmen of all religious
persuasions. I do further declare that neither hopes,
fears, rewards, or punishments shall ever induce me
directly or indirectly, to inform or give evidence against
any member or members of this or similar societies, for
any act or expression of theirs done or made
individually or collectively in or out of this Society in
pursuance of this obligation. This day of our Lord,
March 24th, in the year 1795.

The **Phantom Bride** *crosses the threshold, as the song continues. He turns upstage to face her. She kisses him, and then, with a predatory leap, clamps her bare legs round his waist and her arms round his neck.*

Mary (*singing*)
    ... And is it true? I asked her,
    Yes, it is true, she said,
    For to this heart that loved him
    I pressed his gory head,
    And each night, pale and trembling
    His ghost comes to my side,
    My Harry, my dear Harry
    Comes back to his waiting bride ...

The moon goes behind a cloud. Darkness.

Act Two

Darkness. The lambeg builds to a crescendo. Stops. **Mary Bodle** *cries out. The bodhran sounds more quietly. The moon comes out.* **Mary Bodle** *is sprawled exhausted across the rumpled bed, in a state of undress.* **McCracken** *sits on the side of the bed, equally disarrayed.*

McCracken I must have hurt you. I didn't mean to.

Mary It's a wonder we didn't go clean through the floor.

McCracken It's a tribute to your cousin O'Keefe's workmanship.

Mary God rest him.

McCracken Indeed. For all his freethinking. Are you all right?

Mary We don't hurt that easy. We're a lot tougher than men. (*She touches his shoulder.*) What about you? You're shaking like a leaf.

McCracken The air's a bit chill.

Mary Put your coat round you. Here. (*She disentangles a green frock-coat from amongst the bedclothes, and drapes it round his shoulders.*) They'll not be back this way in a hurry, that's for sure.

McCracken Who won't?

Mary The army, who do you think? Brute men the like of that, imagine it – bloodshed and butchery every day of their lives – and the sight of O'Keefe's promised bride is enough to reduce them every one to whingeing like wee boys.

McCracken I could have sworn to God I saw her myself, down there, in the very house.

Mary   Sure why wouldn't you? Isn't it her house?

McCracken   I can't stand my own mind! The one
thing I always cherished. The men of Reason, logic and
reason, and now I keep seeing the most damnable
things, shadows and moonshine, when I most need to be
clear and true. What have I to do with ghosts?

Mary   There's no escaping them in this townland.
We're well used to the walking dead, we have more
spooks than living bodies round these parts. What of it?
There's no harm in seeing ghosts. There's just no call to
turn into one, before your time. You're still shaking,
what is it?

McCracken *gets up, looks out at the Cavehill.*

McCracken   You can see McArt's Fort now, clear as
day. So that's clear enough, at least. (*He paces about
restlessly.*) It's a curious thing, fear. The soft unbearable
spot on a man's soul. Once touch it, and you've got the
man's price.

Mary   May God forgive you for saying such a thing.

McCracken   He hardly will, though, he'd need to go
into overtime.

Mary   Isn't it fear alone that makes us human? What
else do you think I love you for? Your great doings of
renown? Let your sister idolise you for that, to me it's
just a load of bells ringing . . .

McCracken   It's thought that makes us human, Mary,
the power of thought, the power of the mind. To lose
that, that's what I fear, the one thing.

Mary   It isn't that at all that you fear, nothing like.

McCracken   You think it was fighting, fighting the
battle? That was sheer pleasure, when it came to it.
Clear and unreal as that moonlight. After all the months
and years of muddling and backstabbing and bitterness

and bull, suddenly there we were marching, with an
enemy and a goal, a completely absorbing game, played
out in a dream, you were both in it and detached from
it, watching yourself strike. Fear never came into it, for
me.

Mary Of course not, not with the killing. Why would
that frighten you? It's living that you fear. That's the
sore spot on your soul. Living the way I do, most people
do. Humdrum, ordinary, soon enough forgotten. That's
why you're more in love with that rope than you are
with me and the child ...

McCracken It's not true!

Mary That's why you accepted the command at a few
days' notice, when the sensible men had all gone home
for their tea. That's why you took up arms in the first
place, when you knew in your heart it would spread the
very disease it was meant to cure. And that's why you'll
choose to swing on a scaffold when you could be living
a decent ordinary life in a new country.

McCracken Doing what? Can you honestly see me,
in some Main Street in Massachusetts, behind the
counter of a draper's shop?

Mary Why should that scare you? Weren't you forever
drinking toasts to the great new American republic?

McCracken I belong here. Everything I've done has
been an affirmation of belonging here. How can I leave
now?

Mary Right enough. Especially with the prospect of a
brave and glorious death facing you – dangling from a
rope's end, with the shite dribbling out of your britches.
I'll not be there, Harry. I hope your sister enjoys it. It's
not the worst either. There's what they do to you after
you've long gone, that's still to come. And what's done
in your name.

McCracken   Why can I not live a free life in my own country?

Mary   Why did you allow yourself to resort to the gun?

Pause. **McCracken** *sits down on the top stair.*

McCracken   It was moral force. And then it was physical force. Nobody just suddenly decided that. It was the inescapable logic of events.

Mary   There's always the choice to say no.

McCracken   Saying no is a final exit. You act out your small parts in a huge drama, Mary, but it's not of your own creation. You're acting all along in the dark, no matter how clear it seems at the time. You only have one choice. Either retire from the stage altogether. Or play out all your allotted roles until the curtain falls.

Mary   Aye, that's right. On a stage full of corpses. (*She begins to make the bed.*)

McCracken   It's all I can say. (*The future ghost of* **Jimmy Hope** *enters the downstairs room.*)

Hope   It's no more than we both believed, Harry.

McCracken   Jimmy Hope would have told you better. You would have loved Jimmy.

Hope   The condition of the labouring class was the fundamental question at issue. A man has the natural right to derive a subsistence from the soil in which he invests his labour.

McCracken   I hear you, Jimmy.

Hope   We couldn't reform a system that was rotten at the core. Known activists had been stripped of their livelihoods. William Orr had been hung. We'd been down every road there was and they'd all lead to a dead end. We'd nowhere to go but the whole hog. An independent republic.

McCracken   Most of the men we knew weren't ready to hear you.

Hope   Why wouldn't they be? Weren't they sworn members of the Society?

McCracken   They were merchants first and foremost. Sooner than see their shipping interests threatened, they would have sunk this entire island and every vestige of freedom with it.

Hope   Bad cess to them then, for they're the boys that would put the rope on your neck and on mine too.

McCracken   You're surely not afraid of being hung, Jimmy?

Hope   I ken it's a great honour, but I cannae say I'm dying about it. Any more than you are.

McCracken (*turning back towards the rope*)   I have no desire to die of sickness.

Mary   That's very noble and generous of you. (*Getting back into the bed.*) The love of your family isn't enough. My love isn't enough. You want the love of the whole future world and heaven besides. All right, go ahead, let them love you to death, let them paint you in forty shades of green on some godforsaken gable-end!

She turns her face to the wall.

McCracken (*standing up*)   Mary . . .

Hope   Tone went away to America.

McCracken   Had to go. Indicted for high treason.

Hope   You saw him off, I believe.

McCracken   We took him on a final outing. Up the Cavehill. Up there. McArt's Fort.

Thomas Russell *appears on the forestage, and surveys the auditorium.*

Russell   Isn't it what I'm telling you, mister honey? The storied Athens of the Northern world spread out beneath your feet and fit for the son of God himself would cast his blessed incarnate being into the radiance of it!

McCracken   The Heroic Age arrived that day. Mad keen to fight now. Pledging ourselves for the first time to the republic of United Irishmen. Playing our hearts out.

Hope   And why wouldn't you?

Wolfe Tone *appears beside* **Russell.**

Tone   Hush now, Thomas Russell, with your preachifyin' tongue. Them that knows the spot for their native crib can sooner testify to its true grandeur, and it the birthplace of their natural genius. Henry Joy can tell us the tale, I have no doubt.

McCracken   An August day. Incandescent. Half a dozen of us up there. High as kites.

Samuel Neilson *joins* **Russell** *and* **Tone**.

Neilson   It must be only lofty thoughts do be detaining you on a rare eminence the like of this one, mister honey.

Tone   Isn't it thoughts of our own dear freedom, Samuel Neilson? And the thought that our eyes will never see it, without that England leaves us to our own resources?

Neilson   There's talking.

Russell   She'll never leave this land, I'm thinking, without that we rise up in the red dawn and scatter her scarlet army before us into the foamy tide.

Neilson   And wouldn't we have the right, and the might itself?

Tone   We've been time and again to her front door, with words of reasoning would draw the breath from the philosophers of old. And time and again we've been to her back door, to only beg for a crust in the honeyed words of a decent man of the roads. And haven't we always and ever come away empty-handed, and the murdering red-eyed hounds of the household set upon us to rend us for our pains?

Neilson   There's a pack of curs will run yelping for their kennels and we but slip the leash of the fabled Hound of Ulster.

Russell   Isn't there a kind of glory now rising up among us, to be surveying with a lordly eye the only wonder of the Northern world, like the saints and heroes of ages past? The blue stretch of Lough Neagh like a wondrous county of heaven itself spread out below us, and the elegant neck of the Belfast Lough yearning forward to offer its wild wide mouth to the sea's turbulent kisses, and the sparkling jewel of a town that's in it, a prize the mighty Bonaparte himself would tremble at, and he weighed down with the world's riches?

Tone   Let it not be the prize of a prince or a queen – let it be the sacred realm of the men of no property, and let all this present company vow that we will not rest until we can call it our own dear republic!

Neilson   There's wishing!

Russell   Is there not a dacent mouthful that a man could drink health to such fine talking, and he drouthy with the climbing?

Neilson   Isn't there a choice jug of poteen, cooling in the spring by the fairy stone, for them as wants a sup?

Tone   Do we repair then to oil the ardour of our red mouths with a supeen, and immortalise the whin-scented air with a gallous vision of the future times!

Russell, **Neilson** *and* **Tone** *exit.*

Hope   We hadn't the ghost of a chance. And it takes a ghost from the future times to say as much. It was left too late, Harry.

McCracken   There was a complete chain of military command, right through the North.

Hope   Old maids, the most of them. Cowering under their beds, when it came to the actual killing.

McCracken   I had enrolments of seven thousand Defenders – and that was in Antrim alone.

Hope   How many Protestants had you? (*Pause.*)

McCracken   Well. There was you and me for a start.

Hope   You and me and a handful like me.

McCracken   There were tens of thousands on the roll, only a year or so ago. There was no telling how many would rise.

Hope   We know now, don't we? One thing's for sure, though, Harry. Without the Protestants of the North, there'll never be a nation. Not without them as a part of it.

McCracken   Not without them at the heart of it, Jimmy. Our own people.

Hope   It's the Orange Society has the most of them now. The land was at the nub of it. They were frightened that if the republic came, the Papists would reclaim their ancient lands. It's what some Defenders were thinking too.

McCracken   We never somehow allowed for that in the Mudlers' Club, did we? If the twain but once unite, it is we who shall unite them, God preserve us. With our innocence and our idealism and our cleverness and our dialectic and our heroism. And all the time the brute fact staring us in the face, only we never looked. A field, with two men fighting over it. Cain and Abel. The bitterest fight in the history of man on this earth. We were city boys. What did we know about two men fighting over a field?

Hope It's not beyond resolution. If every man was awarded the equal fruits of his labour – from the land that he works.

McCracken Forget it, Jimmy. They won't listen. Have you ever known them to listen? We got what we deserved. The wild men from the Catholic peasantry – lumped together with a sad rump of bourgeois Presbyterians. The government had it taped. Up to a month before the rising, the magistrates and landlords were attacking the Orange Society as bandits. The next thing you know – they'd taken over the leadership.

Hope It was a handy weapon against us.

McCracken All that would have been forgotten – assuming that we'd won. It's not the British crown that the loyalists are loyal to – it's their own best interests. They're no different from the rest of us.

Hope We hadn't a ghost of a chance. Not as it stood.

Pause.

McCracken You fought a brave fight, anyway. The spartan band. The forlorn hope.

Hope I'm a Templepatrick weaver, and I learnt enough at the reading to read *The Rights of Man.* For the likes of me there's a world to gain, and precious little to lose, Harry.

McCracken For the likes of me, there's even less to lose. There was a linen mill on the Falls, and a printfield in Cromac Square – both of which I bankrupted. They'll be well rid of me in the family.

Hope   Your sister wouldn't thank you for that.

McCracken   Are you still working for her?

Hope   It's changed now, Harry. She was a lady, Miss
Mary-Anne. I'm afraid your brother John's no
gentleman, though.

McCracken   He'll be the big tycoon, that one.

Hope   He gave me the sack, Harry. First chance he
got. He's running the business now, you see. It's a new
age.

McCracken   God Almighty.

Hope   Evil days. Never you fret. The moral force of
the labouring class will prevail, whatever comes or goes.
(*Standing up.*)

McCracken   Don't leave me, Jimmy. There's two
more ages of Harry to sort out. Before that rope teaches
my neck the weight of my arse.

Hope   Sure, I'm years ahead of you. Nothing I can do
for you now, where I am. We'll not meet again now.
No place we can meet now, except in the long memory
of this town, the long dream.

Pause.

McCracken   Exemption granted. You may stand
down, citizen Hope.

Hope *exits.*

McCracken   The steadfast light, the real Northern
Star . . . him. Not me. His was a light that never
faltered. Otherwise, it was penny sparklers and a load of
damp squibs. Goodnight, Jimmy.

He picks up the Night Thoughts *and leafs through it as he
climbs the stairs to bed. He comes across a passage which stops
him in his tracks as he reaches the rope.*

(*Turning to audience.*) Citizens of Belfast ... (*Reading.*) ...

'Now plots and foul conspiracies awake.
And muffling up their horrors from the moon,
Havock and devastation they prepare,
And kingdoms tott'ring in the field of blood.
Now sons of riot in mid revel rage.
What shall I do? Suppress it? Or proclaim? ...'

... as if you had a real choice. Once the sons of riot
get going, the gallant bold Defenders. We let ourselves
get slowly driven into their corner. The age of
compromise, the age of finally taking sides. So much for
the great revolution of United Irishmen. It comes out
looking like just another Catholic riot.

(*He returns to reading the book again.*)

'Self-flattered, unexperienced, high in hope,
When young, with sanguine cheer and streamers gay,
We cut our cable, launch into the world,
And fondly dream each wind and star our friend ...'

Gorman, *a publican from Dublin, puts his head round the front
door.*

Gorman   Will you walk into my parlour, sez the
spider to the fly. (*He crosses to the shelves, takes down a bottle
and two glasses from them.*) I'll have no butty of mine
skulking round my own front door like a tinker's whelp.
Walk in tall and carry yourself like a free man of
Dublin's fair city.

Croaker McFadden *peers tentatively round the front door.*

McFadden (*wheedling*)   You're certain herself is not
maybe at large about the premises, commander?

Gorman   And what would it signify whether she was
or no? Am I to be banjoed in my own snug shebeen by
the likes of her? Name your poison, me ould son.

McFadden (*entering*)   If I've said it before, I'll say it
behind, the commander's not your man for easy

scarifying, amn't I right?

Gorman   It takes something all right to banjo me.

McFadden   I'll have a ball of malt, so. As long as you have the bottle out.

McCracken (*coming down stairs*)   Mr Gorman, how are you this weather?

Gorman   You find me as you left me, Mr McCracken, at your service, sir. Might I present to you Lieutenant McFadden, my aide-de-camp and general factotum.

McCracken   How are you, Mr McFadden?

McFadden   Prepared to do or die, friend – to do or die.

Gorman   Mr McFadden has come on a visit here from me own jewel and darlin' Dublin. He knows me from the ould days when half the agents in Dublin town were altogether banjoed in the hunt for me, till I was approaching the dimensions of the Scarlet Pumpernickel hisself.

McFadden   They seek him here – they seek him there – they seek but they do not find.

Gorman   Divil the finding they'll do, a chara, and me snug in my own little shebeen here in the middle of the county of Antrim, far from where they'd think to look.

McCracken   Your message referred to a business matter, Mr Gorman.

Gorman   It did so, Mr McCracken. A class of business you and me are well versed in, and let them as aren't mind their own. (**McCracken** *glances at* **McFadden**.) As to Mr McFadden here, he himself is a boney fide sworn Defender and fit to be of our company.

McFadden
    Breathes there a man with soul so dead,

Who never to himself has said,
This is me own, me native land!

Gorman   Pipe down, now, with your versifyin', while
Mr McCracken and I proceed with our serious
undertakings.

McFadden   Wasn't I on the very point of withdrawing
into me own counsel, till the swearing-in was overed
with? You have the floor, commander.

McCracken   The swearing-in of what?

Gorman   The matter in hand, Mr McCracken, being
the furthering-on of the grand work you've been doing
for us Catholic Defenders in this country and others to
boot. Notwithstanding which – there being no affiliating
litigation betwixt the twain bodies of men – namely the
Defenders of the one hand and the United Irishmen of
the other – we are conferring upon you a deputy
leadership of the Defenders of this county of Antrim.

McFadden   Spoken from the heart, commander,
spoken from the heart.

Gorman *glowers at him.*

McCracken   You do me an honour, Mr Gorman.

Gorman   Howsomever – to effectuate this presumption
of office – I have first to swear you in to membership of
our society – according to the sanctified precepts of the
national Catholic Defenders of Ireland.

McCracken   I take it that this is the wish of Mr
Magennis?

Gorman   The commandant of the Defenders of this
county of Antrim – the said Mr Magennis – has
empowered me as an accredible deputy – to conduct
this officiation in his unavoidable absence.

McCracken   Very well. What do I have to do?

Gorman All that's needful is to give back the answers to me that's writ on this sheet of paper here. (*Snapping his fingers at* **McFadden**, *who hands over a tattered sheet of paper, which* **Gorman** *presents to* **McCracken**.) Now then, Mr McCracken, friend. 'Do you promise to be true to the present Catholic United States of France and Ireland and every other kingdom now in Christianity?'

McCracken 'I do.'

Gorman 'What is your designs?'

McCracken 'On freedom.'

Gorman 'Where is your designs?'

McCracken 'The foundation of it is grounded upon a rock.'

Gorman 'What is the password?'

McCracken 'Eliphismastis.'

Gorman 'You are now bound fast in the great brotherhood of Defenders. You will know your brother when he joins two hands backwards on the top of his head, lets on to yawn, then draws his hands down upon his knee or the table. You will answer by drawing the right hand over the forehead and returning it to the back of the left hand.'

Gorman *and* **McFadden** *solemnly enact the first sign.* **McCracken** *obediently responds with the latter one. The other two shake him vigorously by the hand, and slap him on the back.*

McFadden Let me shake the fist of a true son of ould Erin, and any bowser that'll not folly suit is me sworn implacable foe, I give fair warning.

Gorman You're a man of honourable standing, Mr McCracken, and I'm telling you now, with the likes of meself at your shoulder, you'll not be banjoed.

McCracken I thank you both.

McFadden   By God I can feel the blood of past ages straining at me weskit buttons, till I could step out now this very minute and tear the throats out of any sixteen Orange craw-thumpers with me bare hands, and be back in an hour for further orders!

Gorman   You'll restrain your ardour till the signal's given by those endowed with a superior sense of conducting themselves in military fashion. Once we're fully riz, there'll not be an Orange cur left in the county with a skinful of life-blood to his name.

McFadden
> Oh the French are on the say,
> They'll be here without delay,
> And the Orange will decay,
> Says the Shan Van Vocht.

McCracken   No. It must be understood that there is no vendetta against the Orange Society. It's true that many lodges have been formed into companies of yeomen by their landlords. They will be sent against us, just as the Catholic militia are, but all those men are the gulls of history. Our quarrel is not with the puppets, our quarrel is with the puppet-masters who pull the strings. The English landed and mercantile interests. That's the power and the only power which we unite to oppose.

Pause.

Gorman   Wasn't I after employing the very self-same form of words as yourself, Mr McCracken, only minutes before your arrival here? Croaker, sez I, if you're after the fellows that's done us the detrimental damage in this country, you need cast your net no further than the English maritime investments.

McFadden   Speaking purely out of me own acquaintance, I'm not afraid to tell whoever's asking, that your Orangeman is as stout a patriot as the next

wan, and a sight more honest than plenty of pious
Papists I could name.

Gorman   Take up your glass, Mr McCracken, and
we'll pour a liberation to the uniting together in your
own good person of our noble and edifying institutions.

McFadden *begins to sing.*

McFadden (*singing*)
   Our cause is just, we shall and must,
   We'll fight and not surrender,
   To plant the tree of liberty
   By united bold Defender ...

Mary *stirs in the bed.*

Mary   Harry?

Gorman   Mother of God, it's herself back early! (*He
snatches the drink from* **McFadden***'s hand, and pours it back
into the bottle.*) Will you quit the catterwailing and get
down out of sight before she's in on us!

McFadden   Hide like a chiseller, is it? Me that's your
boney-fide lootenant from the olden days?

Mary   Harry?

Gorman   Do you hear me, man, make yourself scarce
before we're banjoed altogether! If she finds you loading
into the little store of drink we have left, there'll be a
bloody uprising on these very premises!

McFadden   Loading in, is it? Who invited me in?

Gorman   Well, I'm inviting you back out again.

McFadden   You might explain to your gentleman
Proddy friend, just what the Dublin agent's was after
you for, in the olden days – selling horses that never
belonged to you ...

Gorman   You yella-faced prognosticatin' little gobshite,
I had papers for every last nag of them!

McFadden   . . . interceptin' the unfortunate creatures on their way to the knacker's yard and trying to pass them off as foxhunters . . .

Gorman   By Jasus, I'll obliterate you, you grubby little tinker's bitch!

McFadden *runs into the chorus, pursued by* **Gorman**.
Mary *has got out of bed and come to the head of the stairs.*

Mary   Was I long asleep? Is it nearly dawn?

McCracken   Seven thousand I was promised.

Mary   Seven thousand what?

McCracken   Gallant bold Defenders. Come the day and a hundred-odd turned up.

Mary   Why do you have to keep tormenting yourself? You know the army had them terrorised, in their own homes, long before the rising ever started.

McCracken   That was the only reason I got any of them at all. They told me – we'd rather die like men in battle than be hunted down like beasts of the field.

Mary   You never saw what the army did, you were in prison all during that time. The half-hangings and the pitch cappings. I come up by Muckamore one morning, from the fair. It was a mournful dark mizzly sort of a day, the air was raw. There was a crowd round a cabin where the Monaghan Militia had a man trapped. They'd poured the hot pitch on to his head and set fire to it and shut him in the kitchen with his wife and children. The very minute I drew level, the man appeared up out of his own chimney, he'd scrabbed his way up the inside, he was burning like a torch, and tearing the very scalp off his head, and the molten pitch running down his poor face and him roaring like a wounded heifer, stuck up there with the people all struck dumb watching him, and the soldiers barking away laughing. I put my head down and walked on and tried to rinse it out of my mind, but I'll never lose the sight of it. People can't forget those things.

Pause.

McCracken   People do forget, though. They forget the facts that don't suit them.

Mary   They forget nothing in this country, not ever.

McCracken   No. It isn't true to say they forget nothing. It's far worse than that, They misremember everything. (*Pause.*) Although whether I'm any different I've somehow got to get it straight. Tonight. Just this once.

Mary   The night's nearly gone.

McCracken   It was a fashionable look amongst our members. Cropping the hair short, like the French Jacobins.

Mary   What of it?

McCracken   What do you think inspired their idea of the pitch cap? You think pictures like that aren't seared into my own eyeballs and a million more as hellish or worse, you think prison was a rest cure?

Mary   I know it wasn't.

McCracken   We had the true faith, you see. Reason. The logical men. History was a dungeon. The people were locked into their separate compounds, full of stench and nightmare. But the dungeons couldn't stand against the force of rationalism. Let the people once unite and we would burst open the doors, and they would flood out into the clean sunlight. Heady stuff. Intoxicating. Certainly I was prepared to die for it – but only in the fight against professional soldiers in the field, that was all that we foresaw. We wouldn't even authorise a single assassination, and still they happened in our name in spite of us . . . so all we've done, you see, is to reinforce

the locks, cram the cells fuller than ever of mangled
bodies crawling round in their own shite and lunacy,
and the cycle just goes on, playing out the same
demented comedy of terrors from generation to
generation, trapped in the same malignant legend,
condemned to re-endure it as if the Antichrist who
dreamed it up was driven astray in the wits by it and
the entire pattern of depravity just goes spinning on out
of control, on and on, round and round, till the day the
world itself is burst asunder, that's the handsome
birthright that we're handing on at the end of all . . .

Mary   What use is this?

McCracken   LISTEN TO ME! Fourteen months I
was in Kilmainham gaol. That's where it finally broke
down. The great big new idea. It's not a place for
heroes, prison. Nobody could ever know . . . (*He seizes her
by the hands.*) Just listen to this, you've never heard it, any
of it. We finally ate of the Tree of Knowledge. The
famous poisoned fruit. It was our last and final age. We
introduced each other to it. Shame, Mary . . . (*Leading her
down to a kitchen chair.*) . . . sit down there. (*She sits.*)
Castlereagh came up to Belfast, with a couple of other
lords of the realm, and arrested the whole lot of us.
Except that I was on my way back from a Defenders'
meeting in Armagh. So they intercepted me on the road
and bundled me off to Dublin. I presumed a trial would
follow, but of course it never did. We were held in
solitary for a while. And then herded together.

*The lights have reduced the area round him to a prison cell as he
speaks. The bodhran is beaten, as three other prisoners join him
from the chorus –* **Henry Haslett, Charles Teeling** *and*
James Shanaghan. McCracken *stands on a bench
looking out at the prison yard.* **Shanaghan** *lies prone.*
Teeling *plays patience.* **Haslett** *prowls. The bodhran is
replaced by loud hammering.*

McCracken   There's carpentry for you. You could

hang the whole Four Courts from gallows the strength of those.

Teeling Them carpenters are By Appointment to His Majesty. If you can't expect quality workmanship from the likes of that ... where can you expect it these days, I ask myself.

McCracken You could sing that.

Teeling I often wondered about all that posh food and drink you see in the shop windows, By Appointment to His Majesty. If he appoints to himself all that they're claiming – he must put away a hell of a lot of stuff.

Haslett Why do you suppose he's so fat and dim-witted?

Teeling Could he not maybe arrange to send us a parcel of his leftovers?

Haslett He's not going to send his Gentleman's Relish to the likes of you, Teeling.

McCracken I met yer man at exercise this morning.

Teeling Scant use he has of exercise today. He'll get more exercise than he ever wanted jigging at the end of that rope.

McCracken He was in Belfast working for Charlie Davis the time I was lifted, you know.

Haslett It's damn-all to do with the movement, he's a petty thief, tried and convicted for robbing the mail.

Teeling That's correct. He's not like us. He's an ordinary decent criminal.

McCracken I've only the one regret, he says to me. That I'm to die for a thing I'm ashamed of, instead of for my country's cause.

Teeling It's all one to the hangman, though, when he slips the noose round yer man's neck.

Haslett   Can you not bloody leave it alone, the pair of you! Is it not enough to be cooped up in the shadow of death without your having to drivel on about a hanging like a pair of oul' spey-wives!

McCracken   Don't worry, I can't see them ever topping you, Haslett, you have too much of a brass neck.

Teeling   You can say this for a hanging – it assists in varying the dull monotony of prison routine.

Haslett   Well, you can comfort yourself with that when you're waiting for your own topping. (*He hunkers down moodily on the floor, drawing patterns in the dust with his finger.*)

Pause.

Teeling (*turning over a card*)   The Joker. Maybe there'll be a reprieve.

Shanaghan   Have we had breakfast or not?

Haslett   Is this a time to be thinking of food and a man out there waiting to swing?

Shanaghan   I was trying to remember eating it.

Teeling   You needn't bother, they're holding it back till after yer man's kicked off, when nobody'll feel like eating it. They don't want lags with weak stomachs ruining their good carpets.

McCracken   Come you and keep an eye out, Teeling, the legs are going from under me.

Teeling (*going to help him down*)   Is the oul' rheumatism bad again?

McCracken   Only chronic. (*Getting down with difficulty.*)

Teeling *takes over the look-out.* **McCracken** *sits on the bench massaging his legs.*

Teeling   The rope's going up now. It'll not be long.

Pause.

Shanaghan   What was his name anyway?

Haslett   Whose name?

Shanaghan   Yer man's?

Haslett   What does it matter?

Shanaghan   I've just been trying to remember.

Haslett   You need seeing to, Shanaghan.

A muffled beat starts upon the lambeg.

Teeling   Here they come now, the Governor and the chaplain, practically racing each other to the scaffold.

McCracken   They'll be wanting their breakfasts.

Teeling   Here's yer man, with two screws leading him.

McCracken *starts to climb painfully back up on to the bench again.*

McCracken   Is he bearing up?

Haslett   No doubt he's feeling in the pink, apart from the odd twinge in his neck.

Teeling   Holy Christ. He's saluting us.

McCracken *is up beside* **Teeling** *now. They respond to yer man with clenched-fist salutes.*

Haslett   What the hell are you at, he's only a thieving wee get out to dignify his own insignificance!

McCracken   Would you have us insult a man's courage facing the rope? By God if you had an ounce of his composure . . .

Teeling   The blindfold's on. They're placing him on the trap. There goes the noose.

A roll on the drums. **Haslett** *covers his ears. Silence.* **Teeling** *and* **McCracken** *climb slowly down.*

Shanaghan What is it they call the Governor in here, is it Richardson?

Haslett Will you shut your hole, you stupid bloody curse-of-God halfwit!

Teeling (*to* **McCracken**) How long would you reckon?

McCracken He's a bull-necked sort of a sinner. I'd say twenty minutes anyway.

Teeling They'll let him swing for an hour at least, then.

McCracken More like two, knowing them. It'll be a late breakfast all right.

Lambeg beaten hard. Blackout. Lights up on the four of them huddled on the ground and on the bench, wrapped in blankets. The door is unlocked and a **Warder** *enters, carrying a flat copper pail of steaming water and a scrubbing brush.*

Warder On your feet.

They stand up listlessly, except for **McCracken**.

Warder God, the stench of this cell . . . there's boiling water here and a brush, so get it well mucked out.

Haslett We appreciate the water, thank you, warden.

Warder What's ailing you, McCracken?

Teeling He's been running a fever since Monday, warden, he has the rheumatism all through him.

The **Warder** *prods* **McCracken** *with his foot.*

Warder Stand up, man, I'm talking to you. (**McCracken** *struggles painfully to his feet.*) Are you sure you're feeling sorry enough for yourself?

McCracken Get me a doctor. You've had your sweetener.

Warder   The doctor says he'll see you when you're sick. What the hell's rheumatism, I have it myself right across the small of my back, am I complaining? Anyhow, you'll have room to spread out soon enough, with this pair leaving us.

Pause.

McCracken   Who's leaving?

Warder   The Governor's been seeing deputations. Prisoners' relatives and MPs and bloody Papal Nuncios, for all I know.

McCracken   I wasn't told of this.

Warder   Every man for himself, lad, your friend Neilson's got his bag packed. Compassionate discharge. Haslett and Teeling here are next.

Teeling   You wouldn't just be codding us, warden?

Warder   Did you ever know me to joke? (*Moving to the door.*) I would wish you good riddance. If I didn't think you'd all be back.

Teeling   Was that a joke, warden?

There is a full slop pail by the door. The **Warder** *deliberately kicks it over.*

Warder   Oh, dear. How careless of me. Wasn't it lucky I brought you that water? (*He goes out, locking the door behind him.*)

McCracken   What is this?

Teeling   You know what that bastard's like. He's just trifling with us.

McCracken   Has this been going on behind my back?

Haslett   You know as much as we do.

McCracken   We made an agreement. Nobody leaves this place unless we all leave together.

Teeling   Rest easy, Harry. They're only playing games with us.

Pause.

Shanaghan   I heard a great yarn in the yard, about ... you know, whatsisname. When he was on the run in Leitrim. No, no, not Leitrim ... whatd'yecallit. Roscommon. He was on the run in Roscommon. I think it was Roscommon. It was your man that's always impersonating people. What's his name?

Teeling   McCabe.

Shanaghan   That's it. Yeah. McCabe. His da had that watchmaker's in North Street. Anyway. He was on the run and there was all these Defenders in Roscommon up for trial. So he decided to try and spring them. You know what he did? He dressed up as an English officer and he got that wee man who's the Antrim weaver ... you know, that's always going on about the labouring class ... whatsisname ...

Teeling   Jimmy Hope.

Shanaghan   Yeah, Hope. He got Hope kitted out like an English sergeant, and the pair of them presented themselves at the courthouse in Roscommon and were naturally sat in the best seats in the house. So this Defender called Dry was first in the dock. Guilty, says the judge. Whereupon McCabe gets up and says in his best English accent, M'Lud, I wonder if I might intercede for this unfortunate man?

McCracken   Did Neilson put you up to it?

Haslett   Away to hell.

Shanaghan   The sergeant here and I, sez he, are recruiting for His Majesty. If the prisoner in the dock will agree to enter the king's service for the rest of his natural life, will you release him from the consequences of his evil-doing? By all means, says the judge.

McCracken   The three of you have sold me out.

Teeling   Leave it, Harry, it's not true.

Shanaghan   So whatsisname goes up to the dock and offers this fellow Dry the king's shilling. Dry's mouth falls open, because he suddenly recognises your man, but he gets the hang of the wheeze and joins up. The three of them waltzed out of the court and nobody the wiser. Isn't it rare?

McCracken   United Irishmen indeed – and we don't even keep faith amongst ourselves.

Haslett   We can't put our families in gaol too! If they want to agitate to get us out of this hellhole, how are we supposed to stop them?

McCracken   By telling them. Same as I did. My cousin Councillor Joy is one of the leading advocates in this city, he knows I won't accept favours.

Teeling   You can't blame Sam Neilson's people, Harry. He's the sole support of a wife and three children. His drapery business is closed down, and the presses of the *Northern Star* have been smashed, the man's destitute.

Haslett   He's also seriously ill.

McCracken   Do I look in good health?

Teeling   They'll be letting us all out, I'm certain of it.

McCracken   What's the odds, so long as you're well catered for.

Haslett   In the name of Jesus will you give over? The screw was right, you're a self-pitying, self-righteous face-ache, and I hope to God you rot here while we're safe at home in our beds!

Teeling   Quit it.

McCracken   I don't rank you with the common class

of traitor, Haslett, you're just inadequate. You haven't the strength of character to be the least use to anybody, even yourself.

Shanaghan There was another time he dressed up as a clergyman . . .

Haslett We've heard it, in the name of sweet Christ, a hundred thousand times, the same half-witted yarns, your mind's going, Shanaghan, can you still grasp that, you're a mental case, you're on your way to the funny farm! (*Shaking him by the hair.*)

Teeling Leave him be.

Haslett What's it to you?

Teeling He's doing no harm,

Haslett Don't you come the parish priest with me, you Papish arse-licker!

McCracken Now we're seeing the true colours.

Haslett SHUT YOU THE FUCK UP!

Haslett *picks up the copper pan and throws the scalding water in* **McCracken**'s *face.* **McCracken** *cries out and falls to his knees with his arms over his head.*

Haslett Mr Bloody High and Mighty, see how you like this! (*He beats* **McCracken** *savagely with the copper pan.* **Teeling** *pulls him off.*)

Teeling Quit it, Haslett, quit it!

He throws **Haslett** *to the ground, then bends down beside* **McCracken** *to minister to his wounds.*

Teeling God, you've probably killed him

Pause.

Shanaghan You mind Harry dressing up as a clergyman? When he went and talked that character out of turning king's evidence? You know, in the cell down by the sickroom ... what was his name?

The lambeg beaten. Lights out to black. A white light fades up slowly, directly overhead. The three actors who played **Teeling**, **Haslett** *and* **Shanaghan** *are standing facing the back wall, leaning on their fingertips against the wall, feet splayed out, with hoods over their heads.* **McCracken** *sits on the bench, facing out front, the blanket draped over his head like a shawl.*

McCracken Finish soon now, it must be nearly now, never soon enough, for me to finish, to be finished. First the tight collar of hair, the alleged word of God, spoken at you, over your head, even he needs words, vanity of vanities, faces all around below, swarming for the choicest view. All as in a dream, before the other dream unknown, perchance dreamless. Unknown. Then the man of God safely gone, and the faces, and the black hood, waiting, for the sign. So then the plunge, the wrench, the plunge, the rough strangle, and so there an end. To finish. Unless only to begin anew, there is of course that. Only to glimmer on in the effigy of another time, other times, other effigies, never to know end's mercy, never to be let end, never to know mercy, so much for the rope's comfort, I shall soon be quite enshrined in spite of all. A whore's pox then on the future! And I forgive it nothing, for there's nothing it will learn from those of us who swung for it, no peace to be got from it, for those of us who want nothing more now than to finish, a cat's flux on whatever holy picture they may fashion of me!

Deafening 'white noise' is heard. The three hooded prisoners howl. **McCracken** *covers his ears. An* **Interrogator** *bursts in carrying a baton. He pulls the first hooded prisoner away from the wall, throws him to the ground, and pinions him across the throat with the baton. The noise stops. Rapid crossfire of speech.*

Interrogator Who commanded the rebels in Down?

Prisoner One The Reverend William Steel Dickson.

Interrogator   What happened him?

Prisoner One   He was arrested on June 4th.

Interrogator   Who took over the command?

Prisoner One   George Sinclair.

Interrogator   What happened him?

Prisoner One   He resigned.

White noise. The **Interrogator** *shoves* **Prisoner One**
offstage, grabs **Prisoner Two** *and thrusts him to the ground in*
the same manner. Noise stops.

Interrogator   Who commanded the rebels in Antrim?

Prisoner Two   Robert Simms.

Interrogator   What happened him?

Prisoner Two   He resigned on June 2nd.

Interrogator   Who was appointed to take over?

Prisoner Two   It was meant to be Henry Monro or
John Coulter.

Interrogator   What happened them?

Prisoner Two   They couldn't be found.

White noise. The **Interrogator** *thrusts* **Prisoner Two**
offstage and grabs **Prisoner Three** *as before. Noise stops.*

Interrogator   Who took over from George Sinclair in
Down?

Prisoner Three   Henry Joy McCracken.

Interrogator   Who was given the command in
Antrim?

Prisoner Three   Henry Joy McCracken,

Interrogator   Are you trying to take a hand out of
me?

Prisoner Three   I swear to God, he was made Commander-in-Chief of the whole Army of the North.

Interrogator   When was he made this Commander-in-Chief?

Prisoner Three   Three days before the rising, that's all. June 4th.

McCracken *stands up, throwing off the blanket.*

McCracken   Tomorrow we march on Antrim – drive the garrison of Randalstown before you, and hasten to form a junction with the Commander-in-Chief. The First Year of Liberty, 6 June 1798!

White noise. The **Interrogator** *manhandles* **Prisoner Three** *offstage leaving* **McCracken** *alone, covering his ears. As the noise stops, the lighting returns to normal, and* **Mary Bodle** *runs forward to comfort* **McCracken**. *A blackbird's song is faintly heard, and continues through to the end of the play.*

Mary   Harry! (*She hugs him.*)

McCracken   Is it time yet?

Mary   No. No. Not yet.

McCracken   I can hear a blackbird.

Mary   He's singing in his sleep.

McCracken   Three days to forge a nation in. With a couple of thousand men with pikes. One field piece, that fell apart the third time it was fired.

Mary   Hush, love.

McCracken   We actually had the town sewn up, even so. The cavalry were penned in. Then the men from Randalstown arrived, and met the cavalry clattering down towards them in a fast retreat. Except that they mistook it for an attack and ran like the hammers. The panic spread to my men. They ran too. So that was it.

We were defeated by the enemy's retreat. It's not often you hear that said.

Mary   Come and lie with me, Harry. There's still time enough. Please.

She leads him to the bottom of the stairs. He stops, looks out front.

McCracken   There's a streak of grey in the sky. Over the town. Look.

Mary   The sun won't be fully up for a good half hour yet.

McCracken   You go on up, Mary, I'll follow you in a minute, I promise.

She goes slowly up the stairs, lies down on the bed. He continues staring out front.

McCracken   Why would one place break your heart, more than another? A place the like of that? Brain-damaged and dangerous, continuously violating itself, a place of perpetual breakdown, incompatible voices, screeching obscenely away through the smoky dark wet. Burnt out and still burning. Nerve-damaged, pitiable. Frightening. As maddening and tiresome as any other pain-obsessed cripple. And yet what would this poor fool not give to be able to walk freely again from Stranmillis down to Ann Street . . . cut through Pottinger's Entry and across the road for a drink in Peggy's . . . to dander on down Waring Street and examine the shipping along the river, and back on up to our old house . . . we can't love it for what it is, only for what it might have been, if we'd got it right, if we'd made it whole. If. It's a ghost town now and always will be, angry and implacable ghosts. Me condemned to be one of their number. We never made a nation. Our brainchild. Stillborn. Our own fault. We botched the birth. So what if the English do bequeath us to one another some day? What then? When there's nobody else to blame except ourselves?

He turns and proceeds slowly up the stairs. **Mary** *begins to croon, quietly, 'My Singing Bird'. Dawn is breaking.*

McCracken (*by the rope at the top of the stairs*) There is of course another walk through the town still to be taken. From Castle Place to Cornmarket, and down to the Artillery Barracks in Ann Street. And from thence back up Cornmarket to the scaffold. So what am I to say to the swarm of faces?

He places the noose round his neck.

Citizens of Belfast . . .

The lambeg is loudly beaten, drowning out any further words along with the singing of **Mary** *and the blackbird. Fade lights to black.*

Heavenly Bodies

Heavenly Bodies was first performed (in an earlier version) at the Birmingham Repertory Theatre on 21 April 1986 with the following cast:

Dion Boucicault   Timothy Spall
Johnny Patterson   Sam Dale
Drama students *and all other parts*
Marc Culwick, Marie Francis, Iain Glen, Allison Harding, Paul Kiernan, Paul Mulrennan, Crispin Redman, Hilary Reynolds, Devon Scott, Timothy Watson

Directed by Peter Farago
Designed by Saul Radomsky
Lighting by Benny Ball
Costume by Ian MacNeil
Music by Jim Parker

Act One

16 September, 1890. Morning. The stage of the Madison Square Theatre, New York City. The curtain is up and a worklight is on. The stage is bare except for random bits and pieces of scenery and furniture, which the drama students attached to the theatre have commandeered, for use in particular scenes and speeches on which they have been working.

A class is in progress. A student called **Thomas Belnap** *is declaiming a speech of Faust's from* Faust and Marguerite *by* **Dion Boucicault**. **Boucicault** *himself is the teacher. Three months short of seventy, he sits slumped in a bath-chair, muffled up against the cold and damp in a capacious greatcoat and muffler, with an embroidered smoking hat on his head from which protrude at the sides two tufts of white hair. A second student, a tall and striking dark-haired girl called* **Jessie McDermot**, *sits off to one side, awaiting her turn. The remaining three (or more) students are in a group on the side opposite to her.*

Belnap 'Oh, philosophic fool! Oh miserable pedant, already old – old without ever having known a human joy or human sympathy!'

Boucicault Can't hear you.

Belnap 'Old without a happy memory of youth – the tender thought of love –'

Boucicault For God's sake, boy, speak up.

Belnap ' – the high-souled taste of glory! I will know them yet! I will, if I call unto my aid the Spirit of all evil! The wind rises! The thunder peals! Satan! I invoke thee!'

Boucicault (*startlingly loud*)   SATAN CANNOT HEAR YOU, MR BELNAP!

Belnap (*breaking off*)   May I once again point out, sir, that my throat is inflamed and painfully swollen . . .

Boucicault   What do you expect, you've been abusing it all morning, and me along with it. I suggest we both go home and take to our beds.

Belnap   May I take it from that that I am excused class?

Boucicault   Indeed you may, Mr Belnap. (*As* **Belnap** *is on the point of leaving.*) Don't bother coming back, if you've any sense – except in the unlikely event that you develop a voice one day.

Belnap *sweeps out.*

Boucicault   The wind rises! The thunder peals! And the small rain down it rains for three godforsaken days now, go home the whole crowd of you, I'm not well enough for this.

Students (*a chorus of protest*)   But sir! But Mr Boucicault! I have a speech by heart! We have a scene prepared! What about the exercises? We have two more hours! *etc.*

Boucicault   Enough! My head hurts, my arm hurts, I have nothing to teach you, leave me in peace. Disperse to your homes and batten your doors against the rising flood.

The **Students** *slowly file out,* **Jessie McDermot** *being the last in line.*

Boucicault (*to her*)   Not you.

She turns back, waits. **Boucicault** *sits silent for a moment, turning his eyes up to the roof. The rain can be heard steadily falling on it.*

Listen to it. A flood coming on the land, what does it portend? What is the name of this vile theatre anyway?

Jessie   The Madison Square Theatre, New York City. As you know very well – sir.

Boucicault   Stench. Dank. The sweet, sickly breath of a dark house, I abominate a dark theatre above all things on earth, you have learnt what that means, I hope, to go dark?

Jessie   To close down, Mr Boucicault. No performance.

Boucicault   In which year were you born, Miss McDermot?

Jessie   1868, sir.

Boucicault   I had already been writing plays for thirty years by that time. (*Almost with a sneer.*) Just fancy. I do begin to feel it has been too long a jig. I begin to see the pathos of it. Move me into the light. (*She pushes his chair upstage centre.*) I trust you brought in news from Ireland to read to me today.

Jessie   There's just one item. An obituary. (*Pulling a magazine from her pocket.*)

Boucicault   Not mine, I hope.

Jessie   Hardly.

Boucicault   As a matter of fact, I have always found my previous obituaries very gratifying. The moment they feel assured that you're safely in hell, they'll praise you to high heaven.

Jessie   Johnny Patterson's been killed.

Boucicault   Oh, him.

Jessie   You knew him?

Boucicault   Touched me once for ten guineas, drank it the same night of course, still owes me. The culchie little tinker's get had the temerity to compare himself to me.

Jessie   I guess you don't want to hear this . . .

Boucicault   On the contrary, read it, it will undoubtedly cheer me up.

Jessie (*reading*)   'Johnny Patterson, the Irish Singing Clown, met his death last week in the circus ring in a most untimely accident. He was a devout patriot of his native Ireland, who nevertheless had come to believe that the one hope for that troubled isle lay in a commingling of the Orange and the Green, an accommodation between the Nationalist and Unionist factions . . .'

Boucicault   You have to be a real clown to believe in that.

Jessie   'To this end he wrote a song, "Do Your Best For One Another" . . .'

Boucicault *gives a derisive laugh.*

Jessie   ' . . . which he performed for the first time in the big top of Keely and Patterson's Circus in Tralee on May 27th, holding in one hand a flag showing the harp and in his other, one showing the crown . . .'

Boucicault   Permit me to speculate – abuse hurled from both sides, faction fights ensuing, Patterson set upon by both camps simultaneously.

Jessie   It just says there was a riot, he was trying to save the circus equipment from the mob, and was struck on the head by an iron bar.

Boucicault   Better still. Did he manage an exit line?

Jessie   It doesn't say.

Boucicault   Never knew the meaning of the word exit, the cocksure little scut. No class, you see, no sense of timing. Now when I was starting out in the London theatre, Miss McDermot, there was considered to be only the one correct way to make an exit. You stood up. (*He suddenly and disconcertingly does so.*) You walked to the side. (*He does this also.*) You had reserved the last words of the scene for this move, you thereupon spoke them – and so off. The older actors were lost otherwise, they used to plead with me – 'Dear boy, can't you possibly offer me a few words to take me off, you've left me high and dry' . . . (**Jessie** *smiles; he approaches her.*) You intend to be queen of this castle, don't you, Jessie?

Jessie   I'm here to learn how to act . . .

He leads her to the bath-chair as though to a throne, and hands her into it.

Boucicault   It will not be enough merely to give your body for that crown. (*He crouches over her, fondling her hair and neck.*) It demands possession of your immortal soul. (*He suddenly pinions her in the chair, his face close to hers.*) Look. Out there. What do you see out there?

Jessie   Let go of me, please.

Boucicault   The jaws of the beast, stretched wide, opening up its huge dark gullet to me, oh not to bite, not any longer, it's merely yawning in my face, can you smell it, the breath? The decomposing carcass in its gut? It will swallow me now without even noticing . . .

Jessie   Stop this stupidness!

Boucicault (*breaking away from her*)   I have written for a monster who forgets!

Jessie   You are Dion Boucicault, you are hardly likely to let us forget it nor the public either . . . you are the famous Myles-na-Coppaleen and Conn the Shaughraun, as any passer-by will testify, and you damned well know it!

Boucicault *steps down in front and adopts the demeanour and voice of his character Conn, addressing the audience with the final words of the Shaughraun.*

Boucicault   'She says you will go bail for me . . . You

are the only friend I have. Long life t'ye! – Many a
time have you looked over my faults – will you be blind
to them now and hold out your hands once more to a
poor Shaughraun?'

*And he waits, with winning smile and arms akimbo, for the
automatic applause. Silence. He looks round for* **Jessie**. *She has
slipped away.*

Boucicault   Jessie? Back on stage at once. I want to
hear that speech of Marguerite's. Jessie? (*The distant sound
of the stage door slamming is heard from off.*) NO! (*He rushes
offstage in pursuit.*) Come back here! How dare you leave
me on my own!

*After a moment, he returns to the stage, hunched and frightened-
looking – there's nobody left now for whom to perform. Just the
dark gullet of the auditorium confronting him. He turns, raises his
head, looks right into the blackness of it. With an immense effort,
he switches on the charmlight of his stage persona.*

Dear friends, you have shown this poor old actor great
kindness, yes indeed you have. May I now humbly offer
in return a few lines from a part I composed many
years ago, for the illustrious Mr Charles Kean, later to
comprise one of the greatest triumphs of my dear good
friend Mr Henry Irving . . . and most recently essayed
here in the city of New York by your humble servant.
From Act Four of my *Louis the Eleventh* – the king
addresses his hermit Confessor . . .

(*As Louis XI.*)
   Oh, could you look into my soul, my father,
   My body's anguish is but half my pain:
   The present is a terror, but the past –
   Oh Heaven, I dare not turn and look on that!
   My days are wretched, yet they bring relief
   And come to scare away my nights of terror.
   The gloom takes forms to mock and jibe at me;
   The silence whispers names I loathe and dread;
   And when I sleep, a demon sits and broods . . .

(He is beginning to feel dizzy, and tugs at the neck of his greatcoat.)

   ... a demon sits and broods
  Upon my heart ... a demon sits and broods upon
my ... Upon my heart, I thrust him out ... I
thrust him ... Jessie ... somebody? ... AAAHH!

He stumbles forward in the throes of a heart attack, trying to tear his coat open, and collapses. Transformation. Worklight snapped out, footlights snapped on, music bursting forth. And the ghost of **Johnny Patterson** *rises up from below the stage in an aureole of smoke. He is dressed in his Irish Singing Clown outfit: a baggy tweed suit with shamrocks embroidered on the arms and legs, and a harp on the chest, knee-length white stockings, a conical hat, and a handlebar moustache. There is blood on his forehead and shoulder. He is singing.*

Patterson *(singing)*
  As I was climbin' one fine spring mornin'
  On high Slieve Gullion and the air so sweet,
  I spied above me a poor old woman
  With most of Ireland spread at her feet –
  Upon that vision she was a-gazin'
  Whilst from her eyes there sprang a tear,
  Yet could I hear from that wither'd bosom
  A young girl's voice proud and clear –
  Do your best for one another,
  Not for Erin or the Queen;
  Make your peace with one another,
  Sure we all love our isle of green.
  Though my family be divided,
  Still this land we all must share,
  Do your best for one another –
  'Tis your mother's dying prayer!

Tenderly, he assists **Boucicault** *to arise from the floor. The music turns into a manic jig.* **Patterson** *whirls* **Boucicault** *around the stage, then drops him into the bath-chair and leans over the back of it looking down at him. The music ends.*

Patterson   There you go, Boosy. That's you warmed up.

Boucicault   What has happened? Am I dead?

Patterson   Now you'd hardly be warmed up if you were dead – would you? Naw, you're only dying, like the rest of the population.

Boucicault   What trick is this?

Patterson   Sure it's only Little Johnny Patterson – come to fetch you home for your tea.

Boucicault *starts up out of the chair, moves to a safe distance.*

Boucicault   That song you were singing . . . was it the one that started the riot in Tralee?

Patterson   It was, to be sure.

Boucicault   No wonder they kicked you to death.

Patterson   See now, you're a born comedian. Paddy the Clown!

Boucicault   What do you want of me?

Patterson   One good clown deserves another. You and me, Boosy . . . we're going where the good Paddies go.

Boucicault *forcibly wills himself to rise above the occasion.*

Boucicault   Another time, perhaps. I have my best plays in me still. Heaven will have to endure my absence for a little longer.

Patterson   God, but you're a prize turn . . . as if heaven had any interest in the likes of you and me! We're show people, Boosy. Not legitimate. Heaven is for poetasters and verse dramatists, fellows that paint in watercolours – Englishmen and suchlike. You wouldn't even like it there.

Boucicault   I am unimpressed by hellfire, if that is what you are now threatening.

Patterson   No fear of that, surely – with your Uncle
Charlie a well-connected Church of Ireland minister?
No, no . . . it's a dark little limbo that's reserved for
you, Boosy. A dark and dacent corner of obscurity . . .
altogether removed from off the face of this earth.
Time's up, oul' son. You have been sent for.

Boucicault   NO! I am owed a place in posterity!

Patterson   No such thing. It's not in the contract.
Your soul's not your own, sure you signed it away to
the show business half a century ago.

Boucicault   I was a born poet of Ireland and I
devoted my life to the drama!

Patterson   You were born a chancer and you sold
your gombeen soul to the highest bidder, now – your
three-score years and ten are up, your three or four
entire fortunes duly made and squandered, your three or
four hundred young girls come and gone . . . and the
account's being called in. This way please!

And he sweeps **Boucicault** *across the stage on to the trap,
which begins to descend again.*

Patterson   We're going dark for real now, Boosy.
Down into the dacent dark, like the faithful clowns we
are . . .

Boucicault   WAIT!

The trap stops in its descent.

I demand the rights of a condemned man. I demand a
fair appeal. A review of this case. That is my sacred last
wish. (**Patterson** *is unimpressed.*) Furthermore . . . I am
willing to overlook the ten guineas.

Patterson (*shouting off*)   All right, bring her back up!
(*To himself as the trap ascends again.*) I knew there'd be
trouble with this one. (*To* **Boucicault**.) Stay there till I
tell you. (*He circles round the stage, shouts.*) Stand by for a

reprise! (*To* **Boucicault**.) That's reprise, now, with an 's'
... I did not say reprieve, in case you're wondering ...
right, here we go. Kettledrums!

The drums begin a low roll.

No, no, hang on a mo. (*The drum roll stops: to*
Boucicault.) How far back are we meant to enquire
exactly? Are we to start with the actual night you were
begot? Speaking of things that aren't legit?

Boucicault   There's no call for that!

Patterson   No. I thought you'd sooner skip that, just
as well anyhow, from the management's point of view,
right – we'll simply have to take the plunge and hope
for the best, here we go. Kettledrums!

The drum roll starts again.

DIONYSIUS ... LARDNER ... BOURSIQUOT,
wait, wait, hang on just a minute. (*The drum roll stops.*) I
mean, what the hell class of a name is that? For the son
of a liquor merchant in North Dublin?

Boucicault   Dionysius was a Greek god, as it
happens ...

Patterson   ... and Lardner was a Protestant goat,
right?

Boucicault   Dr Lardner is neither here nor there, I
am the son of Samuel Smith Boursiquot ...

Patterson   You're half a god and half a goat, by the
sound of it.

Boucicault   Samuel Smith Boursiquot, who was the
descendant of a distinguished line of Huguenot
immigrants ...

Patterson   He was a daft oul' codger, if he couldn't
even make a living selling drink to the Irish!

Boucicault   Samuel Smith Boursiquot, who was a

purveyor of fine wines in the city of Dublin ... (*Beginning to step forward.*)

Patterson   That'll do! Contain yourself. I haven't got all day, you know. (*He turns out front again, drawing himself up importantly.*) Right. Here we go. Kettledrums.

The drums begin their low roll again.

Dionysius ... Lardner ... Boursiquot ... (*The drum roll peaks and stops.*) This Is Your Life!

Blackout. Raucous circus music. Flashes of lightning in which **Patterson** *is glimpsed, laughing maniacally and tumbling across the stage. A final flash of lightning and a concluding circus fanfare. Now there is full blackout and stillness, with only the sound of a distant solo violin playing an elegiac air. The light of the morning sun comes slowly up on* **Boucicault**. *His greatcoat, muffler, smoking hat and tufts of white hair are gone. He is instead an elegant young man of the 1850s, rather dandified in his braided frock-coat and floppy bow tie and natty waistcoat and trousers. His hair is dark, thin on top, longish over the ears and neck.*

Boucicault (*stepping forward, adjusting his cuffs*)   My felicitations to the infernal ringmaster. (*Bowing ironically to* **Patterson**.)

Patterson   Glory be, for Boosy is himself again.

Boucicault   Call me Dion.

Patterson   Call me Paddy the Clown.

The unseen **Fiddler** *now makes an appearance, drifting across the back of the stage, a stooped, homeless figure, shrouded in a shabby, outsize ulster. White hair hangs down from under the wide brim of his battered, dark-green hat; his face is hidden from us.*

Patterson   Jumping Jaysus, who's the Phantom Fiddler?

Boucicault   Father?

Patterson   Father ... methinks he sees his da!

Boucicault (*to the* **Fiddler**)　Look at me. Speak to me!

Patterson　If that's oul' man Boursiquot, he never even was your da, let's face it.

Boucicault (*still addressing the* **Fiddler**)　I have earned your blessing long since, you can no longer deny it!

Patterson　And for why would he want to bless his wife's bastard, pray?

Boucicault　That's a dirty slander, I am this man's son!

Patterson　'Course he never should have married a hot little hussy half his age, that's asking for it, but lo! ... the guilty party approaches! The upstairs lodger – the Reverend Dr Dionysius Lardner, a fine fellow-me-lad of Trinity College Dublin ... and the mammy herself along with him.

The **Phantom Fiddler**, *upstage left, stops playing and stands with head bowed as* **Anne Boursiquot** *and* **Dionysius Lardner** *enter from the right. (We recognise them at once, since they are the two students whom we saw in the opening scene –* **Jessie McDermot** *and* **Thomas Belnap** *– simply adopting these two new roles. They and the other students from the first scene will take on all the subsequent roles in similar fashion.)* **Anne Boursiquot** *is in her twenties, flighty and vivacious in a low-cut dress.* **Lardner** *is skinny and bespectacled, and has a piping voice. As they enter, he grabs her from behind, nuzzles her neck, and creeps his fingers lewdly into her décolletage. She nestles back against him, her eyes on her husband.*

Boucicault (*to the* **Fiddler**)　Show your face to him!

Patterson　Oh, yer man is the Protestant goat all right ...

Boucicault　STRIKE HIM DOWN!

But the **Phantom Fiddler** *stays where he is, bent and still;*

and **Boucicault** *falls to his knees, burying his head in his arms.*

Anne (*pushing* **Lardner** *away*)   It is no longer in doubt, Dr Lardner. I am carrying your child. I demand to know your intentions towards it.

Lardner (*gesturing at the* **Fiddler**)   Would the daft oul' codger acknowledge the brat as his own, d'ye suppose?

Anne   He will know all too well that it cannot conceivably be his.

Lardner   Not conceivably, no indeed. (*With a little snigger.*)

Anne   The Boursiquots are, however, a respectable family. Samuel will of course treat the child as his own in the names of propriety and decorum.

Lardner   Grand and glorious names, the pair of them. (*And he entwines her in a lascivious embrace.*)

Boucicault   Cockatrice, usurper! Goatsucker!

Patterson   D'ye mind?

Boucicault   Crock-full of cant and cuckoldry!

Patterson   Some of us are trying to watch this, you know. (*To* **Anne Boursiquot**, *who has just broken free of the embrace.*) Carry on, love.

Anne (*to* **Lardner**)   Is it your desire to continue lodging in my house?

Lardner   The accommodation is agreeably commodious, Mrs Boursiquot.

Anne   I shall require two undertakings. One, that you act as guardian to the child with respect to schooling and career. Two, if it prove a boy child, his given names shall be ... Dionysius Lardner.

Lardner   Is that entirely advisable?

Anne   It is my desire, Dr Lardner.

Lardner   Then it certainly must and shall be fully satisfied.

Anne (*opening her arms to him*)   Dionysius!

Lardner (*grabbing her*)   Mrs Boursiquot!

Patterson   The Age of Steam – and no mistake.

The **Phantom Fiddler** *strikes up an anguished cadenza on the violin, and then exits left as* **Lardner** *sweeps* **Anne Boursiquot** *off on the right.*

Boucicault   It's none of it true!

Patterson   You know, if this Lardner fella had only been your uncle . . . you could maybe have played Hamlet instead of the clown. D'ye get it? Ach, get up out of that and quit the catterwailing, it was you that ordered a recount.

Anne (*from offstage*)   Dion!

Patterson   You hear that? Smarten up and act your age, the mammy wants a word with her little lad.

Boucicault, *still on his knees, straightens up and dries his eyes like a small boy.* **Anne Boursiquot** *enters, goes to him.*

Anne   Dion pet, what are you doing out here, have you been crying, there now, mammy's here . . . (*She cuddles him, kisses his head – he hugs her, still on his knees.*) Guess what, pet – Dr Lardner has a birthday present for you. Look.

Lardner *appears, wreathed in steam from a model traction engine which he is carrying. He sets it down so that it puffs its way towards* **Boucicault**.

Lardner   Steam, my boy – Steam! The greatest power on God's earth, and it's mine and yours to exploit. (*He picks the model up again.*) What do you have to say to that?

Anne   Dr Lardner is an authority on Steam. Dr Lardner has written an encyclopaedia. In one hundred and thirty-four whole volumes! Just imagine.

Lardner   Tell me, Dion, how would you like to be filthy rich and a power in the land, eh? Whenever you're a big boy?

Anne   Dr Lardner is going to apprentice you as a civil engineer!

Lardner   You shall assist me to design a railway – all the way from London to Birmingham, my boy. What do you have to say to that?

Boucicault (*sullenly*)   I want it to come through Dublin.

Lardner   I fear the little man has been missing his geography lessons.

Anne   Indeed he has not, have you pet? He loves school. Tell us what you did in class today, go on, love. What was the lesson today?

Boucicault   Drama.

Anne   Drama? Isn't that grand, Dr Lardner? Was teacher reading a little play to yous all?

Boucicault   We were acting out a story . . . it was a real good story, it was a man called Oliver Goldsmith, he made it all up, like . . . only teacher wanted us to act out a story of our own after that . . . so I sat down with my jotter . . . and I started to write, Mammy . . . you see, I was making up a story of my own, guardian . . . and I kept on writing and I never stopped, when my ink ran out I switched to pencil, and after a while, before very long, I stopped and looked, and there it was, I wrote a play, I wrote a play, I WROTE A PLAY MOTHER!

Music. He leaps to his feet, as they cower before his onslaught.

The magick to conjur spirits, to strike clowns dumb, to amaze princes and emperors, I have it in me, stronger than any steam, you insufferable little swindler . . .

Lardner *turns on his heel and rushes out, and* **Anne** *runs after him.*

Boucicault (*as they vanish*)   . . . that's what I learnt in school today, since you ask.

Patterson   So much promise in one so young.

Boucicault   Telling stuff, though, you have to admit. For a schoolboy of sixteen.

Patterson   Oh, telling is the word all right.

Anne (*a cry from off*)   Dion!

Patterson   There's the mammy at it again.

Anne (*off*)   Dion, please, where are you?

Patterson   Out here on the stage, missus.

Anne (*re-entering*)   That man has torn the heart from my breast . . . he has taken my life-blood . . .

Boucicault   Skedaddled?

Anne   My life is over! (*She collapses into her son's arms.*)

Boucicault   I knew all along he'd abandon you.

Anne   He has run away to London, with the wife of Captain Heaviside!

Boucicault (*with dawning delight*)   Sweet God above us . . . Heaviside? His partner? He's six foot six . . . he's a Guards captain. He'll break every spidery bone in that cocksure body!

Anne   Oh no, don't, I couldn't bear it if he was hurt . . .

Boucicault   Him? Hurt? That lecherous viper? That steam-inflated huckster?

Anne   I will not have any more language, Dion.

Boucicault   That shabby, shoddy little charlatan, that

pip-squeak, that wife-plunderer, that shrivelled lump of cold steamed cod-piece, how can you even bear the touch of that smug slimy goat-sucking jumped-up quacksalver of a SCIENTIST, Mother, how?

Anne Oh, God, look at your eyes ... you're the very spit and image of him!

Boucicault NOT TRUE!

Anne I love him and I want him!

The **Phantom Fiddler***'s tune is heard from off.*

Boucicault Power is all he wants and he's got bored with wielding it in this house ... listen to me, Mother. Lardner is across the water now for good. My father, who is to this Hyperion to a satyr, is here at home in Ireland ... let Pappy back into our house now, give him a chance ...

Anne (*striking him furiously*) You little fool, you know nothing! You have learnt nothing! Boursiquot is a worthless poltroon, a pathetic, puny excuse for a man ... never speak his name to me again!

She storms out, as the fiddle music stops abruptly.

Boucicault (*calling after her*) Tell me where he lives at least, I need to know him ... (*Turning to* **Patterson**.) Right. I want Lardner back out here immediately.

Patterson No need to shout. I'm working on it.

Boucicault I shall play Captain Heaviside myself in this instance.

Patterson It's only right – sure your acting's always been that way.

Boucicault Meaning what?

Patterson On the heavy side.

Boucicault Music.

During this exchange, **Boucicault** *has been pulling on a false beard and donning a top hat and opera cloak, from a costume trunk which is part of the stage furniture. Piano music begins. The parlour ballad, 'O That We Two Were Maying'.* **Lardner** *appears, playing the piano (or miming at an invisible one) with* **Mary Heaviside** *standing at his shoulder. They are singing the duet.*

Lardner *and* **Mary Heaviside**
  O that we two were maying
  Down the stream of the soft spring breeze . . .
  Like children with violets playing . . .

Boucicault *assumes his role as* **Heaviside** *by thumping at their hotel-room door; the singing abruptly ceases.*

Lardner   Who is it?

Heaviside   Make your peace with God, Lardner.

Mary Heaviside   Merciful heavens, it is Richard!

Lardner   Be quiet, woman, or we are lost.

Mary Heaviside   But what shall we do?

Lardner   Hide yourself. Quickly!

Mary Heaviside   Where, in God's name?

Lardner   Anywhere . . . under the piano.

Heaviside   Don't oblige me to smash the door before I start on you, Lardner.

Lardner   Go on, go on . . . (*Pushing* **Mary** *under the piano. Calling.*) Just one moment.

With **Mary Heaviside** *crouching under the piano,* **Lardner** *opens the door to her husband.*

Lardner   Why, Richard. How agreeable. What brings you to London?

Heaviside   The overnight packet, Dionysius, and then a team of horses . . . helped along by this. (*And he produces*

*a horsewhip from under his cloak and cracks it in the air,
advancing on* **Lardner**.)

Lardner   My dear fellow ... what on earth has got
into you?

Heaviside (*calling*)   Mary! Which hole has this scuttling
little cockatrice hidden you in?

Lardner   You must be labouring under some
extraordinary misapprehension, Richard ... aaagh!

Heaviside *has started whipping him on the buttocks. He races
round the piano, pursued by* **Heaviside**, *who finally catches him
and pinions him over the keyboard.* **Mary** *gives a little scream
from underneath the piano.* **Heaviside** *pauses, glances down.*

Heaviside   Ah, there you are, darling, I wondered
where you'd got to. Come and join us. (**Mary** *crawls out,
very cowed.*) Do forgive my interrupting your music-
making. You absolutely must oblige me with a ballad.
Try this one. (*Indicating a song in the book on the music stand;
and then cracking the whip to get them started.*)

Mary *plays the piano while* **Lardner** *rather hoarsely sings.*
Heaviside *sits a little way off giving* **Lardner** *a taste of the
whip at the end of every other line.* **Patterson** *meanwhile does a
grave little dance to go with the song.*

Lardner (*singing*)
Do not trust him, gentle lady,
Though his voice be low and sweet,
Heed not him who kneels before thee
Gently pleading at thy feet.
Now thy life is in its morning,
Cloud not this, thy happy lot,
Listen to the gipsy's warning,
Gentle lady, trust him not –
Listen to the gipsy's warning,
Gentle lady trust him not.

Lardner *and* **Mary Heaviside** *scuttle off, and*
Boucicault *discards his* **Captain Heaviside** *get-up.*

Boucicault   Such a satisfying scene . . . almost as though I'd written it myself.

Patterson   Ah, I dunno – it wasn't that bad.

Boucicault   It put paid to Lardner at any rate, and may hell roast him now and for evermore amen.

Patterson   Excuse me – but he went on paying your allowance notwithstanding.

Boucicault   My training as an actor was paid for by my mother's cousin, Arthur Guinness.

Patterson   Arthur Guinness? Not actually . . . *Arthur Guinness?*

Boucicault   He was involved in the brewery trade.

Patterson   We're all quite aware of his trade, thank you. Arthur Guinness . . . sure my wife frequently claimed I was married to the same man.

Boucicault   My mother's side were all wealthy Protestants from the North of Ireland.

Patterson   Oh well, 'nuff said – a thespian type, christened Dionysius, from the wrong side of the blanket, was the one thing they'd always wanted for Christmas, am I right?

Boucicault   Once Guinness discovered the true nature of my vocation, I was disinherited, destitute . . . Dispossessed, as my father had been before me . . .

Patterson   Not the Phantom Fiddler again, in pity's name, will you try at least to move this along a bit. Come on! You tramped the English provinces.

The dialogue suddenly accelerates to Fast-Forward.

Boucicault   I tramped the English provinces, as a jobbing actor, using the name Lee Moreton as a *nom-de-théâtre*, until I fetched up in London, in a garret at Charing Cross.

Patterson   The ink froze in your inkwell.

Boucicault   The ink often froze in my inkwell, I was forced to climb into bed fully clothed, and continue writing in pencil . . .

Patterson   There was luckily plenty of lead in your pencil . . .

Boucicault   . . . working away all night underneath the blankets.

Patterson   . . . as many a piece of fluff will bear witness.

Boucicault *clutches his forehead, sways a little, and the pace returns to normal.*

Boucicault   What are you doing to me? Where am I?

Patterson   You have planted your foot in the heart of the British Empire's stage . . . and said, 'This spot is mine'.

Boucicault   What is the name of this theatre?

Patterson   What, this? This is London's own famous Covent Garden Theatre, Boosy . . . (*A free-standing theatre stage door has appeared.*) . . . the cathedral of the legitimate drama in England. You beat a pious pilgrimage to its door often enough, in your Lee Moreton days. (*Knocks on the stage door.*) Until one day they finally let you in.

The door is whipped open and a hawk-faced stage **Doorman** *looks out; the pace hots up again.*

Doorman   Soliciting is prohibited, whether from hawkers, beggars, pedlars, ponces, would-be players or self-styled playwrights, thank you and good morning.

Boucicault *plants a swift foot in the door before it can be closed.*

Boucicault   Good morning, my card. (*Presenting it.*)

Doorman (*glancing at it*)   Mr Morton. One hour late.

Boucicault   Late for what?

Doorman   Step in please.

Boucicault steps through the door, the **Doorman** *closes it and presents* **Boucicault** *with a written note.*

Doorman   From Mr Charles Matthews. Whom I shall now apprise of your entrance.

The **Doorman** *exits.* **Patterson** *darts forward to read the note over* **Boucicault***'s shoulder.*

Boucicault (*reading*)   'My dear Maddison' . . . oh, good God.

Patterson   What's going on?

Boucicault   The doorman has misread my card, he thinks I'm Maddison Morton instead of Lee Moreton.

Patterson   Who's this Maddison Morton?

Boucicault   A famous author of farces.

Patterson   Tell us this – are you making it all up as you go along?

Boucicault   I could never presume to compete with my own life for sheer inventiveness.

Charles Matthews *enters. He is in costume as the Hunchback of Notre Dame, and is engrossed in reading a manuscript. He doesn't look up at* **Boucicault**.

Matthews   Y'know, I have a definite hunch about this play . . . the hiding under the piano, Maddison. It's a bit improbable, even for a farce, don't you think so?

Boucicault   Mr Matthews . . .

Matthews   Mmm? (*Glancing up; double-take.*) Great heavens – you're not Maddison Morton. You're not even a grown man.

Boucicault   Mistaken identity, at the door, sir, tried to explain, got rushed on in, most embarrassing . . . off I go . . .

Matthews   What brought you here in the first place?

Boucicault   Fact is, sir – I submitted a little piece of my own some months back, under the name of Lee Moreton.

Matthews   I see, I see, look here my boy, we are inundated with plays, I fear, far more than we can ever read, I shall have my secretary return your script. How is it entitled?

Boucicault   *A Lover By Proxy*, sir.

Matthews   I beg your pardon?

Boucicault   *A Lover By Proxy*.

Matthews, *astonished, examines the title page of the script in his hand.*

Matthews   How supremely droll . . . look here, Mr Moreton, it is the very play I have been reading! Yes, look, 'by L. Moreton Esquire', I assumed it was Maddison's, I have misread your name just as my doorman did!

Patterson   This is so ridiculous, I'm nearly inclined to believe it.

Boucicault   Might I dare hope for a production, sir?

Matthews   A production? (*Richly amused.*) Oh lord no, dear boy, there's no possibility of that. The British public no longer believes in farces.

Boucicault   What do they believe in now, Mr Matthews?

Matthews   Circuses.

Patterson   Surprising how sensible the British can

sometimes be.

Matthews *tosses the script to* **Boucicault**.

Matthews   Never mind, we're all square now, cheerio! (*And he makes to leave.*)

Boucicault (*in desperation*)   Tell me, sir, what kind of play do you most long to read?

Matthews   Oh, a thumping good five-act comedy of modern life, I imagine ... (*And he is gone.*)

Boucicault *prowls around the stage, as the action returns once again to a walking pace.*

Boucicault   It was all I needed to hear. Farquhar, Congreve, Sheridan, Goldsmith ... Comedy of Manners! Wit, elegance, refinement of feeling, a wise and genial exercise for civilised minds, the very art I most humbly aspired to practise!

Patterson   Comedy be damned, all that high-falutin antiquarian repartee ...

Boucicault   What in hell would you know, you insignificant pig-ignorant pratfall-merchant!

Patterson   Such wit and elegance, such refinement of feeling ... and furthermore you never did nothing humbly from the day and hour your mother relieved herself of you.

He has knocked on the stage door again, and the **Doorman** *opens it before* **Boucicault** *can get a reply in. The action accelerates once more.*

Doorman   Tinkers, tailors and tarts need not apply, likewise aspiring actors and dramatists, foundlings, and the mothers of foundlings, thank you and good afternoon.

Boucicault *thrusts an even speedier foot in the door.*

Boucicault   Good afternoon, my card. (*Giving it to him.*)

Doorman (*glancing at it*)   Mr Boucicault. Never heard of you.

Boucicault   Pray tell Mr Charles Matthews I have something to give him.

Matthews *has wandered on, once again in his Hunchback costume.*

Matthews (*to the* **Doorman**)   Is that the postboy?

Boucicault (*calling*)   Me again, sir, saw you four weeks ago, said you wanted a five-act comedy of modern manners, am now in a position to supply same.

Matthews   The Irish boy, is that it?

Boucicault   May I come in?

Matthews   Morton, wasn't it?

Matthews *has come as far as the door, so that* **Boucicault** *is able to reach past the* **Doorman** *and thrust his script into* **Matthews**' *hands.*

Boucicault   For you, sir.

Matthews   Good lord, whatever is this? ... (*Reading.*) '*Out of Town*, A Comedy in Five Acts' ... do you mean to say you have composed this since I saw you the other day?

Boucicault   Such as it is, sir.

Matthews   Most remarkable.

Patterson   Entirely nauseating.

Boucicault   Might you have the time to consider it, sir?

Matthews   Well ... why not? My wife Madame Vestris and I are reading scripts over the weekend, we shall try your little effort out on our house guests, Mr Morton.

Boucicault   Actually, sir, it's Boucicault – Dion
Boucicault.

Matthews   Aha, you have adopted a fancy stage
name, isn't it rather a mouthful, though? Never mind,
dear boy, it certainly sounds more theatrical than
Charles Matthews, what?

He exits laughing and the **Doorman** *promptly shuts the door in*
Boucicault*'s face. The action slows down again.* **Boucicault**
stalks around the stage grim-faced.

Boucicault   He sprawls out on his ottoman in front of
a glowing hearth, snorting into a large cognac, Madame
resplendent in her latest gown, the distinguished guests
disposed about the warmly-lit room . . . and outside, in
the dark empty yawn of an indifferent world, you prowl
the streets, incapable of rest, dispossessed and starving.
You pass and pass and press your face against the
window, devouring the picture of them in there, plump
with wit and wine, their flesh creamy with pleasure as
they breathe in the intoxication of their own fame and
power . . . power over you and all your kind! You stare
in till your eyes are burnt hollow, watching them idly at
play upon your name, upon your parentage, at play
upon your provincialism, at play upon your PLAY! and
all the while the monstrous ache, the lust you feel, to be
let in, to burst the muzzle and gorge down the entire
room, by Christ I would cheerfully kill the goatsucker,
and eat the floral tributes off his hearse SINGLE-
HANDED!

Patterson   A wise and genial exercise for civilised
minds . . .

And **Patterson** *knocks on the stage door, which is whipped open*
as before by the **Doorman**. *The pace accelerates.*

Doorman   Stage-door Johnnies, Champagne Charlies,
Hooray Henrys and Jack-the-Lads not admitted, thank
you and good evening, oh, it's you, sir.

Boucicault   By appointment.

Doorman   Step in, please, I shall apprise Mr Matthews of your entrance.

Boucicault   Do so. (*As he steps through the door.*)

Doorman   But soft – he approaches.

The **Doorman** *unctuously departs as* **Matthews** *appears, still the Hunchback and still clutching the script.*

Matthews   Boucicault, my dear boy, permit me to dissipate your anxiety on the instant – Madame and I are enchanted with your piece, so much so that we have resolved to put it into production forthwith, you must come and read it to the company next Friday. There will of course be alterations necessary, but you must excuse me or I shall miss my entrance!

He thrusts the script into **Boucicault**'s *hands and rushes off. And the bells of Notre Dame peal out in joyful din.* **Boucicault** *raises his arms to heaven in thanksgiving, throws himself down, drums his heels on the floor, rolls around laughing hysterically – then leaps to his feet. The bells abruptly stop.*

Boucicault   What alterations?

Patterson   Ah, Jaysus – I've got that terrible yawn you get in the large intestine, when somebody says, this is where the story really begins.

The backdrop parts, to reveal **Charles Matthews**, **Madame Vestris** *and the members of their company standing in a line and applauding. They have been listening to* **Boucicault** *reading aloud his play. He moves up towards them, having reached the final speech.*

Boucicault (*reading*)   'Max Harkaway: Permit me to correct you on one point. Bare-faced assurance is the vulgar substitute for gentlemanly ease; and there are many who, by aping the vices of the great, imagine that they elevate themselves to the ranks of those whose faults alone they copy. No, sir! The title of gentleman is the only one out of any monarch's gift, yet within the reach of every peasant. It should be engrossed by Truth – stamped with Honour – sealed with good-feeling – signed Man – and enrolled in every true young English heart.'

The company, wreathed in smiles of approval, applauds with gusto.

Madame Vestris   Bravo, indeed, and now off to the greenroom with us all, to toast our brilliant young scribe with a glass of champagne. Lead the way, Mrs Nisbet.

They all stroll off chatting excitedly, except for **Matthews***, who draws* **Boucicault** *aside, and* **Vestris***, who hangs back also.*

Matthews   Now then, my young lion, how are we to make this piece of yours work on the stage?

Boucicault   Sir?

Matthews   Let us consider my own character, merely as an example – it won't do to have him Irish, you know, won't do at all. It means playing him as a garrulous buffoon . . . let him be droll, let him scintillate! We really mustn't call him Mulvather. Make him English! Let us call him – Dazzle.

Boucicault   Pardon me, sir . . . but that is already the name of Mr Farren's character. Sir William Dazzle.

Matthews   Quite so, dear boy – you must find a new name for Billy's part also, but not to worry, there's time enough for that.

Madame Vestris *(intervening)*   Dion, my darling, this title, *Out of Town* – it's much too homespun for such a momentous debut, it makes the wrong emphasis, the title should rather proclaim your arrival in our midst, your triumph over wild and primitive origins, it should hoist your banner, you are assured of a great success in the premier theatre in England – what do you say to *London Assurance?*

Boucicault (*to* **Patterson**)   Get them off.

Patterson   Are you talking to her or to me?

Matthews   How clever, darling. Absolutely! *London Assurance*!

Boucicault   Get them off, for God's sake!

Patterson   All right, they're going, they're going.

And the backdrop closes again, shutting **Matthews** *and* **Vestris** *out.*

Patterson   The fact remains – she certainly got your number very nicely with that title.

Boucicault   It was still my own work at the end of all!

Patterson   Did I say it wasn't? Even if you did walk out on the opening night?

Boucicault   I was a boy of twenty. I couldn't bear it out there, in the lap of the beast, I fled away into the dark ... I found myself on Waterloo Bridge, in the rain, my cheek was pressed against a wet stone balustrade, to try and quench the fire in it ...

Patterson   You had caught a germ in the blood, Boosy, that sudden terrible doubt – maybe I'm not the genius I thought I was up till eight o'clock this evening. Farquhar, Sheridan, Goldsmith – Irishmen all, but conquerors of the English stage – and taking over the torch now, Dionysius Lardner Boucicault! Quote – 'Mr Boucicault's *London Assurance* is the legitimate heir of *The Recruiting Officer, She Stoops to Conquer, The School for Scandal* ... in brief, he is the authentic comedy genius of the Age' ... that was what you were petrified they wouldn't say, am I right?

Boucicault   I walked back to the theatre, it was ringing with laughter and cheers. I rushed in, the place was jammed, I saw the final scene, there was a cataclysm of joy, I was manhandled on to the stage to receive the roar of the beast, the curtain descended for the final time. I was engulfed in rapture!

Patterson   Yeah, I know the feeling.

Boucicault   You? You have no idea what I'm talking about, don't try to compare the circus ring with the legitimate stage!

Patterson   Fine word, legitimate.

Boucicault   I was acclaimed as the great rising dramatic poet of the Age!

Patterson   Now, gods, stand up for bastards.

The backdrop parts again, to reveal the London Assurance *company holding their final bow, and then straightening up from it.* **Charles Matthews** *steps downstage towards* **Boucicault**.

Matthews   My dear boy. The gods have indeed smiled upon us. The heavens beckon. Speak your heart to us.

Boucicault   I am struck dumb.

Matthews (*taking him by the hand*)   Come. (*He leads* **Boucicault** *up to* **Madame Vestris** *and* **Mrs Nisbet**.) There. Does not the company of angels inspire you to eloquence? What do you have to say to your leading ladies?

Boucicault *puts his arms round the two women's waists.*

Boucicault (*ravenously*.)   KISS ME!

Vestris *offers up her mouth, and he falls upon it, then upon* **Nisbet**'*s. The band strikes up a triumphant intro, to 'The Garden Where the Praties Grow' – then continues on to the first line, which* **Patterson** *sings.*

Patterson
Have you ever been in love, my boys,
Or did you feel the pain . . .

The band stops. **Boucicault** *has finished kissing* **Mrs Nisbet** *and is shaking hands with the other members of the company as they drift off. He is finally left with* **Matthews**, *who draws him into a private colloquy. All this is happening upstage as* **Patterson** *continues with his patter and singing.*

Patterson   I had a pal once worked in a freak show. The Living Skeleton – that was his billing. He was a vegetarian drinker – he would drink anything out of a bottle so long as it wasn't milk or beef tea. But the best of it is – his name was Coffin! I kid you not. Mickey Coffin.

The band resumes, he sings.

I'd rather be in gaol myself
Than be in love again . . .

The band stops, he speaks.

Mickey the Living Skeleton and me came from the County Clare. Born in the same village, the same year, 1840. Growing up with the same stench. Sweet sickly breath on the land. By the time we were nine all the other boys were dead of hunger – potato blight they called it – so Mickey went out on the road as a Living Skeleton, and as for me – I wrote this song.

The band resumes, he sings.

Though the girl I loved was beautiful,
I'd have you all to know
That I met her in the garden where the praties grow!

End music. **Matthews** *has now followed the company off.* **Boucicault** *rejoins* **Patterson**.

Boucicault   What do you mean plaguing the stage with all that?

Patterson   Just practising me act. I got tired of watching yours.

Boucicault   My life is the one in the balance! Yours is already consigned to limbo and you're more than welcome to return to it.

Patterson   Will we go, then?

Boucicault   As it happens, I'm only just getting started.

Patterson   'Permit me to correct you on one point: the title of gentleman is the only one out of any monarch's gift, yet within the reach of every peasant . . .' Tell us, Boosy – how many peasants have you actually met? I'd say that I'm your first and last, and speaking for Mickey Coffin and me, you can stick your title of gentleman, we'd sooner be seen dead, thanks.

Boucicault   You're a peasant snob, Patterson. You think to be poor and to suffer is a superior state of being, mouldering away in some boghole in Connacht, but there is no shred of virtue in being a victim – history disables all of us, in whatever fashion, it's the use to which we put our disabilities, that's virtue – not how much we suffer them – it's how we act upon them!

Patterson   So tell us, Mr Boucicault, how did you react during the Great Irish Famine? – Oh, I kept London well supplied with me comedies of manners.

Boucicault   As opposed to being a clown in a travelling circus, let's say?

Patterson   I kept faith with my own people, as a true clown should.

Boucicault   And I kept faith with my own work, as a true artist must, to make a living thing that endures . . .

Anne (*calling from off*)   Dion!

Patterson   There's the mammy arrived from Dublin.

Boucicault (*still to* **Patterson**)   . . . a thing that endures – that is the sole redress we have, against history and all its crimes.

Patterson   You can speechify, Boosy – but you've been a clown all along and a false one at that.

Anne Boursiquot *enters, in coat and hat.*

Anne   Dion dearest!

Boucicault (*going to her*)   Mother!

Anne (*embracing*)   Oh, my little lad, you have worked such wonders! But you needn't have sent us so much money.

Boucicault   I have a house in Pembroke Square, Mother. I have a carriage and two horses, I wanted you here to see it all for yourself.

Anne   I'm so relieved you've given up the acting, pet, it had my entire connection scandalised.

Boucicault   Listen to me, Mother. This is only the start. A New Age is on the rise, and my star along with it, it's the birth of opportunity for anybody with the determination to seize it, irrespective of who you are or where you come from. I have planted my foot in the heart of the Empire's stage, and said – This spot is mine!

Anne   You're the mirror image of Dionysius, every word you utter could be his!

Boucicault   Don't mention that little goatsucker's name.

Anne   I hope you've written and told him your good fortune.

Boucicault   I want my father's address, I want him to know, I want him to see my play, where is he?

Anne   You know very well that Boursiquot has been dead to me for fourteen years past!

Boucicault   He may be buried somewhere in Ireland, but he is not yet quite dead, just tell me where he works.

Anne   Go home and find him for yourself, if it means so much to you!

She turns on her heel.

Boucicault   Mother! (*She pauses.*) On Monday night my new play opens. *The Irish Heiress*. I have arranged for you and William to have the best seats in the house.

Anne   Your brother is arranging accommodation, I must join him. (*She walks on out.*)

Boucicault   But you'll be staying at Pembroke Square . . .

Patterson *has produced a newspaper with an ostentatious flourish. He reads aloud from it.*

Patterson   'It was interesting to observe whether the author had progressed . . . whether he had elevated himself to something like a position as a producer of dramatic literature . . . *The Irish Heiress* is not an advance. It is as much a farce as *London Assurance*, and it is a weak farce instead of a strong one. There is the same want of creative power, but there is not the same buoyance and spirit; there is the similar selection of well-tried means, but the same taste is no longer employed, and the result is feeble and inefficient.'

Boucicault   Are THEY down there?

Patterson   To whom do you refer?

Boucicault   Them – those wens and warts, those goitres on the throat of poetry, those styes in the eye of inspiration, those tapeworms of a theatrical culture . . .

Patterson   The actors?

Boucicault   The critics!

Patterson   Oh, the critics, oh yeah – the critics are all down below all right, you can certainly count on that.

Boucicault   In which case do your damnedest, but you will never contain me in any hell I have to share with them. They crucified me!

Patterson   Excuse me, but that would have put you in a different league altogether.

Boucicault   Every play I offered was violated by them, mocked, debased, trampled into the dirt.

Patterson   They were only doing their job, sure the public had no stomach for all that fustian backchat.

Boucicault   Oh yes, the roar of the beast, that too ... I was writing comedy of manners for a people who had passed beyond manners, beyond comedy. A New Age on the rise, oh yes ... plunder and pig-ignorance, a New Dark Age of blood force, the likes of Lardner with his scientific baubles, millions enslaved by them, a raw-boned British master-race, clothing their barbarism in piety and pinstripes and fairy-princess sugar candy, what entertainment does such an age demand, do you suppose?

Benjamin Webster (*suddenly entering*)   Melodrama, Dion. The people want melodrama.

Webster *is a theatre manager, raw-boned, British and dressed in pinstripes.*

Boucicault   Enter Benjamin Webster.

Patterson   So which theatre is this?

Boucicault   The Haymarket in London. He's the proprietor.

Patterson (*to* **Webster**)   How'd y'do?

Webster (*oblivious to this*)   The French, Dion, look at the French. Boulevards ahead of us, in the melodrama stakes. Why not pop over to Paris and see what you can gather up?

Boucicault *has sat down with a mirror and a make-up box at the moment of* **Webster***'s entrance, and has begun to transform himself into* **Alan Raby***, the title role in his play* The Vampire. *He continues with this throughout the scene that follows, with* **Patterson** *acting as his dresser.*

Boucicault   Listen, Webster. I laboured for six months over *Old Heads and Young Hearts*, you can afford to pay me more than one hundred pounds for it, damn you!

Webster   Market forces, Dion. Personally I subscribe to the Free Trade League, I mean look at it with common sense: I can pop over to Paris, see how a play is taking the stage, invest twenty-five pounds in a translation, and presto – I have a hit. Whereas some unknown quantity of yours is going to mean risking hundreds. I mean, *Old Heads and Young Hearts* is a sound enough comedy in its way . . .

Boucicault   Charles Matthews and Madame Vestris will get three thousand a year for appearing in it!

Charles Matthews *enters.*

Matthews   It will not run for a week, dear boy, let alone a year.

Madame Vestris *follows him on.*

Boucicault   Certainly not the way you're playing it, Matthews. Having engineered your own bankruptcy, you now appear determined to achieve mine.

Matthews   My dear boy, with your brute appetite for houses, clothes and carriages, along with gaming, wining, dining, whoring and borrowing, you are entirely self-sufficient in that regard.

Madame Vestris   Our author has a young head. With a very old heart.

Boucicault (*to* **Webster**)   They are perfectly entitled to write a play, but they are not entitled to write my play!

Madame Vestris   We took your wild scribblings and fashioned them into a play called *London Assurance*, that is our business, though you have soon enough forgotten it.

Boucicault   Your business is to utter what I create, I want no one's opinions but my own as to the consistency of my characters.

Matthews   Very well, you shall have none but your own. As from now, you no longer have a company.

Matthews *and* **Vestris** *stride off.*

Webster   I shall of course persuade them to stay on, at a price. As for you, Dion – it's back home to the bog, I'm afraid.

Boucicault   They would never have treated Oliver Goldsmith like a hired clerk!

Webster   Tell me something – did you study French at school as well as Oliver Goldsmith?

Boucicault   My French is impeccable.

He has now finished making himself up as the vampire, with 'livid face and fixed look' (Queen Victoria). **Patterson** *helps him into the* **Alan Raby** *cloak and tunic – with the chained bible hanging from the belt – during the next speech.*

Webster   Here then is my offer. Set up shop in Paris. For every play you purloin and re-fashion, I shall pay you fifty pounds. I have even taken the trouble to draw up a contract. (*Producing it from his inside pocket.*) You should clear three thousand a year quite comfortably.

Boucicault   So. You have gone so far as to calculate my price.

Webster   Merely the price of the style in which you are now accustomed to live. There is of course the artistic option, ink frozen in the inkwell, obscure and bitter penury, all that kind of thing.

Boucicault (*taking the contract*)   Very well, Webster.
I shall sell myself into perdition. Watch out for the free
market, though. One day it may be me who is buying
you. (*And he signs the contract on* **Patterson***'s bent back.*)

Webster   Oh, absolutely, Dion.

Boucicault *hands over the signed contract to* **Webster** *who
pockets it and departs.*

Webster (*as he goes*)   Much obliged.

Patterson (*shouting into the wings*)   Right you are, he's
sold himself! To the highest bidder! You can give him
the girl now, go ahead, send her on!

Vampire wedding music. Snow-covered mountains appear. Enter
Anne Guiot – *from* **Boucicault***'s* The Vampire *in a filmy
wedding dress and veil.* **Boucicault** *has become* **Alan Raby***.*

Raby   At last. She is here. Tonight, ere the moon
rises, a new life drawn from the pure heart of a maiden
must enter into this form. Her life for mine!

Anne Guiot (*French accent*)   What do I hear?

Raby   You hear that I love you. Anne, my soul, are
you not mine?

Anne Guiot   What power is this that oppresses me?

Raby   It is my will; mine eyes fix upon thy heart as if
with fangs, while my soul like a serpent entwines thine
within its folds, and crushes thee to my will. Anne, thou
art mine!

Anne Guiot   Spare me. Yes, thou art my master; I
cannot oppose thee.

Raby (*taking her by the hand*)   You are robed for the
altar . . . I will take you there. (*He begins leading her up the
mountainside.*) My will beckons thee to come.

Anne Guiot   I obey. I obey . . .

Raby   She is mine!

As they reach the mountain peak, the macabre wedding music wells up. **Raby** *lifts back* **Anne**'s *veil and bends down as though to kiss her – but instead sinks his teeth into her neck. She gives a deathly cry and falls off the mountain out of sight.* **Raby** *turns his bloodstained mouth and outstretched arms in triumph towards the new moon rising. Then, as the music peaks, he sweeps back down. The lights change, the music finishes, and* **Boucicault** *is once more standing in front of his make-up box and of a mirror held by* **Patterson**, *wiping the blood off his mouth.*

Patterson   So. Are you going to tell us or not?

Boucicault   Tell you what?

Patterson   Did she fall off that mountain or did you push her?

Boucicault   Neither.

Patterson   You're not pretending you were never married to a French heiress?

Boucicault   For a time I was. A brief time.

Patterson   So how did she die?

Boucicault   Like most people. By degrees.

Patterson   You mean there was nothing perpendicular to it?

Boucicault   That rumour was a journalistic fiction from start to finish.

Patterson   Although she didn't exactly leave you hard up.

Boucicault   She belonged to the nobility.

Patterson   Nice going, Boosy. She was your very first adaptation from the French – am I right? Tell you one thing – she was a lot easier to credit than some of them other melodramas you brought back with you.

Boucicault   All I did was honour the bond, to supply the beast with all its orders . . . lust, greed and sadism framed around with hearts and flowers . . . a faithful mirror of the Empire.

Patterson   You loved it!

Boucicault   Melodrama was the raw fuel of the age, nothing less – crude and explosive like the base culture it energised, it is literally child's play, if you've ever bothered to observe children play-acting, I was obliged to cater to childlike minds! Charles Kean's amongst them.

Patterson   Ah holy God, spare us another flint-hearted theatre manager.

Boucicault   He had the biggest hits in his career from me, it was of no account, I was still the pariah, beyond the pale, unworthy.

Patterson   For what?

Boucicault   For Agnes Robertson, what else . . . his darling ward and protégée, the most breathtaking girl of nineteen I had ever laid eyes on.

Patterson   And you've laid eyes on a few.

Boucicault   I played the vampire to her sweet English virgin . . . my own play, my own production, we took Kean's theatre by storm!

The vampire music again. **Patterson** *flees into the wings.* **Boucicault** *turns back into* **Alan Raby**.

Raby   Now for my new bride. Agnes! Agnes, arise! – she obeys me. Come, I command thee! – so, she approaches – she is a slave to my will!

Enter **Agnes Robertson**, *in a trance and a flimsy nightdress.*

Agnes   I am here.

Raby (*making to embrace her*)   Agnes . . .

Agnes   Touch me not, thy touch strikes cold into my heart – oh, let me sleep.

Raby   Why do you look thus upon me?

Agnes   Begone! You inspire me with terror.

Raby   Thou lovest me, thy soul is mine, come to my heart, thou can'st not escape the spell my spirit has cast upon thine. Why do you repulse . . .

Agnes   Because that breast upon which you press me seems to be the bosom of a corpse, and from the heart within I feel no throb of life!

Raby   Ah! Dost thou know me, then?

Agnes   Away – Phantom! Demon! – Thy soul is dark, thy heart is cold.

Raby   Agnes – thy life must pass into that heart.

Agnes   Avaunt! – leave me! – my father . . . my guardian . . . oh, my voice is choked with fear . . . avoid thee, fiend! Abhorrent spectre . . . !

He kisses her; she returns the kiss.

Raby   She is mine!

And he buries his face in her neck, as she clutches him in a passionate embrace. As the music ends and the lights change, they disengage from the embrace, with **Boucicault** *now playing himself again.*

Boucicault   My fiery little star . . . It is not yet too late to change course, you know.

Agnes   You may change, Dion. I know now I never will.

Boucicault   Your guardian believes there is no room for my like in civilised society.

Agnes   It's only because you're a vampire.

Boucicault   He informed me that you were his ward, that you were betrothed to the Earl of Hopetoun, and that my employment with him was hereby terminated.

Agnes   What did you say?

Boucicault   I said, actually Mr Kean, it goes like this – the Earl of Hopetoun is a joke. You are an old woman. Agnes is affianced to me. We both hereby resign.

Agnes   He'll do all in his power to separate us.

Boucicault   New York is beyond his power, Agnes, and the power of all his kind . . . a mansion of the dispossessed, for generations of my own people, a place of transfiguration, I'm going to forge myself a new soul in a new world, and you along with me!

Agnes   Dion, surely it could be arranged for us to travel out together . . .

Boucicault   I've already told you. There are certain affairs that I have to settle, before I go.

Agnes   What affairs?

Boucicault   My father's.

The **Phantom Fiddler***'s music is heard.*

Agnes   I can wait for that . . .

Boucicault   However – the work in New York will not wait for you, you have to go there at once, Agnes.

Agnes   I should like to meet your father.

Boucicault   So would I, but I don't think you'd like the look of him.

Agnes   How can you say that . . .

Boucicault   He's been dead since April.

Agnes   My poor Dion . . . how so?

Boucicault   It appears he had been working in a brewery all these years . . . in the town of Athlone, it's dead in the centre of Ireland, furthest away you can get from any coast, more or less. I expect he felt safe there. I wanted his blessing on my work . . . I seem to have frightened him. Do I frighten you?

Agnes   I do sometimes wonder if you really are a vampire.

Boucicault   Of course I'm not, not during daylight hours.

Agnes   You never see daylight, the way you live.

Boucicault   I shall be seeing a lot more of it than I care for, between Liverpool and New York.

Agnes   So shall I, Dion – between New York and you.

She kisses him lightly and exits. He looks after her, lost in thought. The **Phantom Fiddler** *appears upstage, as before, playing away.* **Boucicault** *sees him, moves up towards him.*

Boucicault   Father . . . have you no word to say to me?

The **Fiddler** *suddenly swings around. He has a death's head.* **Boucicault** *cries out in fear and falls down in a dead faint.*

Phantom Fiddler   This is my beloved son, in whom I am well pleased – HEAR YE HIM!

And with a bloodcurdling laugh, he whips off the hat and skull mask to reveal himself as **Johnny Patterson**. *The band strikes up with 'The Garden Where the Praties Grow'.*

Patterson (*singing*)
Have you ever been in love, my boys,
Or did you feel the pain,
I'd rather be in gaol myself
Than be in love again,

Though the girl I loved was beautiful
I'd have you all to know
That I met her in the garden where the praties grow!

The band stops. But the **Phantom Fiddler***'s lament
continues faintly throughout the following speech.*

Funny you should mention Liverpool, Boosy – it was the
first place I ever sang that song. I'd only just finished
writing it, on the road, with Pablo Fanqué's circus.

(*Sings unaccompanied.*)
    She was singing an old Irish song,
    Called 'Gradh Geal mo croid-he' . . .

(*Speaks.*) It was an entirely Irish audience in Liverpool,
that night, most of them still speaking the ould tongue.
They'd come over twenty years previous. Driven out.
Refugees from the Famine.

(*Sings unaccompanied.*)
    Oh boys, says I, what a wife she'd make
    For an Irish lad like me . . .

(*Speaks.*) I was orphaned very young, I grew up with the
smell. My uncle enlisted me, I was a drummer boy, I
marched with the regiment, along by the ditches piled
high with misshapen corpses, with the mouths stained
green from eating grass and docken.

(*Sings unaccompanied.*)
    I was on important business but I did not like to go,
    And leave the girl and garden where the praties
        grow . . .

(*Speaks.*) The praties. The taties, the spuds . . . the
potatoes. That was what failed, Boosy, every garden a
family grave, sick-sweet and stinking. Little children like
stick effigies. Mumbling on the shrivelled dugs of
mothers scarcely adult, already senile. Famine . . . not a
man, woman or youngster in that audience whose
destiny wasn't ordained by it, who hadn't lost a mother,

father, brother, sister, husband, wife, sweetheart, country, why? Why? WHY?

The fiddle music abruptly stops.

(*Sings rapidly, still unaccompanied.*)
    She was just the sort of creature, boys,
    That nature did intend
    To walk straight through the world, my boys,
    Without a Grecian bend
    Nor did she wear a chignon, I'll have you all to know
    That I met her in the garden where the praties
      grow . . .

(*Speaks.*) I sang on to the end, and I heard neither laughter nor jeers, but a long low moan – the keen of grief for the phantom generations with us there in the tent – and I felt the humility and privilege of my clown's motley, and was proud.

The band strikes up the tune again.

(*Full performance.*)
    Says I, my pretty fair maid, I hope you'll pardon me,
    But she wasn't like those city girls that would say,
      'you're making free',
    She answered me right modestly and curtsied very low,
    Saying, 'you're welcome to the garden where the
      praties grow' –
    She was just the sort of creature, boys,
    That nature did intend
    To walk straight through the world, my boys,
    Without a Grecian bend –
    Nor did she wear a chignon, I'll have you all to know
    That I met her in the garden where the praties grow!

The band stops. **Patterson** *goes over to where* **Boucicault** *is lying, and hooks him under his armpits in order to hoist him to his feet.*

Patterson So you see, Boosy, we've had enough of vampires, the country's life-blood sucked dry . . . time to turn in now, come on, let's shift!

The band strikes up a demented version of the fiddle air.
Patterson, *holding* **Boucicault** *under the arms from behind, dances him round the stage and on to the trap, which begins to descend, with* **Patterson** *roaring with laughter as* **Boucicault** *struggles helplessly in his arms. Lights fade to black.*

Act Two

From below the stage, **Boucicault** *and* **Patterson** *ascend once more on the trap.* **Boucicault** *is middle-aged now, bald on top, morose. He is on his knees.* **Patterson** *is brushing him down.*

Patterson There you go, Boosy. There's no harm done. (*Raising him to his feet.*) That's you to rights. You're as right as rain again.

Boucicault I do not consider rain to be the epitome of rightness.

Patterson *Touché*, very rich! – and you thinking you were a goner there, just for a bit.

Boucicault It appears you are entertained by playing the fool with me.

Patterson Sure playing the fool is the one talent we have, you and me both . . . naw, it was just a little false alarm to gee you up a bit, I mean, no harm intended but I do have a matinee today.

Boucicault What do you mean? You can't still perform?

Patterson Divil the bit else, it's part of the deal. All your celebrated performances, Boosy – you'll be repeating them all, ad infinitum, only difference being, there's no exits any more . . . and no audience, of course. That's the meaning of limbo in the show business. On for the duration, all by yourself, no earthly stars and no heavenly bodies . . . just this. Are you ready for it yet?

Boucicault *moves away from the trap.*

Boucicault I can smell blood.

Patterson   Where can we be?

Boucicault   New York City, where else.

Patterson   Your favourite theatre!

Boucicault   Far more than just a theatre – a non-stop street carnival, a world's fair, a bazaar of the nations, an adolescent girl's heart with the head of a brutal businessman!

Patterson   Did you write that or was it for real?

Boucicault   Wall Street. (*Produces a notebook, consults it.*) The crash of 1837. A crooked banker is on the point of defaulting on his debts. His name – is Gideon Bloodgood.

Agnes *enters, pushing a baby carriage.*

Agnes   I thought I would show little Eve her very first theatre.

Boucicault *is trying out the role of* **Bloodgood**.

Boucicault   So, as I expected, every stock is down further still, and my last effort to retrieve my fortune has plunged me into utter ruin . . .

Agnes   Dion!

Boucicault   But all is prepared for my flight with my only care in life, my only hope, my darling child, her fortune is secure . . .

Agnes   Oh, it's something you're writing! For a moment I took you seriously.

Boucicault   That's not like you, Agnes. (*Looking into the baby carriage.*) Well, little Eve – it's no garden of Eden here, is it? Look at her, she's a perfect image of you. A proper Fairy Star.

Agnes   I hate them calling me that.

Boucicault Are you feeling any stronger today, Agnes?

Agnes Strong enough to come this far . . . what do you mean?

Boucicault Tomorrow New York will ring from Union Square to the Battery with the news – Bloodgood has absconded!

Agnes You surely can't want me to start again already?

Patterson *suddenly takes over the* **Bloodgood** *role.*

Patterson Yonder street, now so still, will be filled with a howling multitude, for the house of Bloodgood the banker will fail, and in its fall will crash hundreds, thousands, who have their fortunes laid up here . . .

Agnes Dion, I can't face the road again, not yet.

Boucicault But tomorrow I shall be safe on board the packet for Liverpool!

Agnes We had four continuous years of it – I know what you are going to say, I was on stage again within the month after little Willie's birth, but I have two of them to cope with now . . .

Boucicault All I asked was, are you feeling stronger? Apparently you are. Where is little Willie, by the way?

Agnes Zoe took him to the circus.

Patterson Good on you, Zoe.

Boucicault Has Zoe mentioned giving notice at all?

Agnes I thought you'd paid her.

Boucicault Paid her, dear? What would I pay her with?

Agnes You still have the play on, *The Invisible Husband*.

Boucicault This theatre is dark, Agnes, you passed

the notice on your way in, *The Invisible Husband* closed last night.

Agnes   Oh, no . . . I'm so sorry, Dion.

Boucicault   What the public actually wants to see is the Invisible Wife – their very own Fairy Star.

Agnes   Such a stupid title to be given . . .

Boucicault   Nothing less will suffice. She's the darling of the gods, and better yet, of the dress circle. But we aren't going to let them have their Fairy Star until she's strong enough (*Kissing her forehead.*), are we, dear?

Agnes   It's only really the touring. If we could remain here just for a while . . .

Boucicault   Not another word, we shall doubtless find some way to survive, like all the poor of New York.

Agnes   One more week, Dion. Then I'll start back, I promise.

Boucicault   Only if you feel up to it, Agnes. Little Eve is frowning at me.

Agnes   I must go, it's time she was in bed.

Boucicault   Goodnight, my child. See you tomorrow.

Agnes *exits pushing the baby carriage.*

Patterson (*as she goes*)   But tomorrow I shall be safe on board the packet for Liverpool!

Boucicault   First complication. Bloodgood is about to flee with cash in hand, when his bankruptcy is discovered by his rascally clerk Badger. Badger tries blackmail. Bloodgood tries bribery.

Patterson *continues doing* **Bloodgood**'s *lines, whilst* **Boucicault** *takes on the role of* **Badger**.

Bloodgood   Mr Badger!

Badger   Mr Bloodgood!

Bloodgood   I have been deceived in you. I confess I did not know your value.

Badger   Patience and perseverance, sir, tells in the long run.

Bloodgood   Here are three thousand dollars – I present them to you for your services.

Boucicault   Further complication. An old seadog called Fairweather has that very day deposited his life's savings, one hundred thousand dollars in cash, in Bloodgood's safekeeping. He now bursts in upon them . . .

Enter **Fairweather**.

Boucicault   . . . having heard rumours that Bloodgood's bank is about to crash, demands the return of his money, and thereupon keels over in a fit of apoplexy.

Fairweather (*keeling over*)   I am suffocating – some air – I cannot see – everything is black before my eyes. Am I dying? O, no! no! it cannot be. Some water – quick! Come to me – my wife – my children! Where are they that I cannot fold them in my arms? (*He looks strangely and fearfully into the face of* **Bloodgood** *for an instant, and then breaks into a loud sob.*) Oh, my children – my poor, poor little children! (*After some convulsive efforts to speak, his eyes become fixed.*)

Bloodgood   Someone run for help. Badger, a doctor, quick.

Badger (*standing over* **Fairweather**)   All right, sir, I have studied medicine – that is how I learned most of my loose habits. (*Examines the captain's pulse and eyes.*) It is useless, sir. He is dead.

Bloodgood   Dead! Can it be possible?

Badger *tears open the captain's vest and the receipt for the* *money falls to the ground.*

Badger   His heart has ceased to beat – apoplexy – the cause is natural, over-excitement and sudden emotion.

Bloodgood   Dead!

Badger   You are spared the agony of counting out his money.

Bloodgood (*the cunning realisation*)   Dead . . .

Badger (*spotting the receipt*)   Ha! Here is the receipt! Signed by Bloodgood. As a general rule, never destroy a receipt – there is no knowing when it may yet prove useful. (*Pockets it; then, in his own voice.*) They remove the captain's body to the street . . . (*Gestures impatiently at* **Patterson**, *who drags* **Fairweather** *offstage.*) . . . they then disappear about their business. So much for Act One. Acts Two and Three, assorted pathos and romance amongst Bloodgood's victims – and so to Act Four. Badger reappears as a reformed character, at last prepared to expose Bloodgood by means of the receipt – which he has carefully hidden under the floorboards of his tenement room. Unable to find it but determined to destroy it, Bloodgood resorts to desperate measures – he sets fire to the entire house. And thereby creates an absolute sensation.

Behind the back wall and before our startled eyes, the scene unfolds in the way that **Boucicault** *imagines it will.*

Boucicault   Stage dark. The exterior of the tenement house, $19\frac{1}{2}$ Cross Street. Through the upstairs shutters, the light of a flame can be seen, rising, dying down, reviving. The door is cautiously opened. Bloodgood lets himself out.

Patterson/Bloodgood *emerges from the door.*

Patterson   In a few hours, this accursed house will be in ruins. The receipt is concealed there – and it will be consumed in the flames!

Boucicault The glow of the fire is seen to spread from room to room . . .

Patterson Now, Badger – do your worst – I am safe! (*He exits.*)

Boucicault The house is gradually enveloped in fire . . .

Music. The fire begins to crackle and roar. Cries from off – 'Fire! Fire!' as an alarm is sounded. Several citizens rush on and mill about in agitation, watching helplessly as the fire spreads.
Boucicault/Badger *pushes his way through them, kicks in a ground-floor window, climbs in and disappears. A young* **Onlooker** *rushes after him.*

Onlooker Stop! Stop!

The **Onlooker** *leaps through the window, but soon re-appears, face black with smoke, coughing; he collapses into another citizen's arms. The shutters on an upper window fall to the ground and reveal* **Boucicault/Badger** *struggling through the flames on the landing; but there is a loud crash and he disappears from view, as though falling with the inside of the building. The onlookers cry out in horror.* **Boucicault/Badger**, *dragging himself from the ruins, falls out across the ground-floor window sill. Two of the onlookers, recoiling from the heat, pull him clear. He holds aloft the receipt in triumph: Tableau. The fire fades away. Everything goes to blackout as the music ends. A single match is struck,* **Boucicault** *lights a cigar. The lights slowly come up again on him and* **Patterson**, *who has sidled back on.*

Boucicault So there it was. I had secured an audience. That was what it took, in the new age, in the new world. Creating the illusion of fire in a crowded theatre.

Patterson Hot stuff, Boosy.

Boucicault They got their money's worth. I went on to invent fireproof scenery, as it happens.

Patterson There was nobody, you might say, who

could hold a candle to you. You were a second Dr
Dionysius Lardner!

Boucicault   Lardner's dead and gone and bad cess to
his memory, it has nothing further to do with me.

Patterson   All that trickery ... you took after him as
a wizard of applied science, amongst other things.

Boucicault   I was an artist obliged to use whatever
tools there were to hand, you think I can't tell the
difference between poetry and hokum?

Patterson   Search me.

Boucicault   The theatres of the day were chock full of
guano, by public demand. I was obliged to shovel it in,
along with all the rest of them, fine – but there was a
crucial difference between my dung and theirs, which is
why it made more money than anybody else's – my
dung had more integrity.

Patterson   It was universally acknowledged as the
genuine article.

Boucicault   Listen to me, Patterson. Latent in every
age there is a Homer, Virgil or Dante. The question is
whether the age desires to draw them forth or not. The
Victorian Age has higher aspirations than these – it
demands that Michelangelo market a cheaper sewing
machine, it obliges William Shakespeare to write for
some scurrilous daily rag!

Patterson   Won't wash, Boosy, them was the boys that
rose up above their times, instead of bowing and
scraping and pandering ...

Boucicault   I confronted the major issues of the day!

Patterson   Such as?

Boucicault   The Indian Mutiny, for one.

Patterson   That was good for a laugh.

Boucicault   Negro slavery for another.

Patterson   What was your view of it?

Boucicault   I was against it.

Patterson   Africa salutes you.

Boucicault   You think that was easy, in America, on the eve of the Civil War, to stage a play with a slave heroine?

Patterson   It did you no harm at the box office anyhow.

Boucicault   I knew in my bones the meaning of enslavement and dispossession, I carried the stigmata of a supposed child of nature, of an artist amongst the barbarians, of a licensed song and dance man for the British Empire, that was why I gambled everything on that play! Every cent I'd earned had been spent on the Winter Garden Theatre, I'd only opened it two months previously, if *The Octoroon* had failed I would have gone under . . .

Patterson   So that was why you ended it with the paddle steamer on stage blowing up and burning away to blazes?

Boucicault   What of it?

Patterson   You were a right little pyromaniac, weren't you?

Boucicault   I engineered sensations. There had to be a sensation scene, every time, public demand, the beast was ravenous for it.

Patterson   You see, I was different from you, Boosy, I actually *liked* the audience.

Boucicault   Up until the night they kicked you to death.

Patterson   I died trying to tell them what they didn't

want to hear. You told them all the lies they longed for
– in return for which they loved you to death.

Boucicault   It was me who gave the voice of Ireland a
hearing on the stages of the world, which it had never
before received in all its tormented history!

Patterson (*singing*)
  Erin, the smile
  And the tear in thine eye . . .

Boucicault   I wrote *The Colleen Bawn* and the genial
spirit of Oliver Goldsmith danced at last down
Broadway with me!

Patterson   Ah, the darlin' Colleen Bawn!

Music. During the song, **Boucicault** *dons the coat, hat and
boots of Myles-Na-Coppaleen, loveable rascal and comic hero of*
The Colleen Bawn.

Patterson (*singing*)
  Oh, if I was the Emperor of Russia to command,
  Or Julius Caesar, or the Lord Lieutenant of the
    Land,
  I'd give up all my wealth, my means, I'd give up my
    army,
  Both the horse, the foot, and the Royal Artillery;
  I'd give the crown from off my head, the people on
    their knees,
  I'd give my fleet of sailing ships upon the briny seas,
  And a beggar I'd go to sleep, a happy man at dawn,
  If by my side, fast for my bride,
  I'd the darlin' Colleen Bawn!

Music ends. **Boucicault** *steps forward with a prop whiskey
barrel on his shoulder and addresses the house as* **Myles-Na-
Coppaleen**.

Myles   Long life to yez all!

Patterson *steps smartly into the role of* **Corrigan**, *a
conniving attorney.*

Corrigan Who's there? Why, 'tis that poaching scoundrel, that horse stealer, Myles-na-Coppaleen – with a keg of illicit whiskey, as bould as Nebuckadezzar. (*Approaching* **Boucicault**.) Is it yourself, Myles?

Myles No – it's my brother.

Corrigan What's that on your shoulder?

Myles It's a bolster belonging to my mother's feather bed.

Corrigan Stuffed with whiskey?

Myles How would I know what it's stuffed with? I'm not an upholsterer.

Corrigan Come now, Myles, I am not the mean creature you imagine.

Myles Ain't you now, sir? Still, you keep up appearances mighty well, just the same.

Corrigan I am not that blackguard I have been represented.

Myles I see your true character, sir – you're another sort of blackguard entirely.

Corrigan Myles, you have come down in the world lately – and it's the love of Eily O'Connor that's in it – it's the pride of Garryowen that took your heart away and made you what you are – a smuggler and a poacher.

Myles Oh, murder – Eily, aroon, why wasn't ye twins, and I could have one of ye, only nature couldn't make two like ye – it would be onreasonable to ax it.

Agnes *appears, in the role of* **Eily O'Connor**, *accompanied by* **Hardress Cregan, Eily**'s *secret husband in* The Colleen Bawn.

Eily Poor Myles, do you love me still so much?

Myles Eily, if tears were poison to the grass, there wouldn't be a green blade on Glenna Hill this day.

Eily Myles, you saved my life – it belongs to you. There's my hand, what will you do with it?

Myles *takes* **Hardress**'s *hand and clasps it together with* **Eily**'s.

Myles Take her, wid all my heart.

Tableau. A resounding fanfare. **Patterson** *becomes the master of ceremonies once again.*

Patterson Her Royal Highness The Queen Victoria And Her Consort The Crown Prince Albert, who's knocking at death's door, so keep it bright and keep it brief!

Fanfare again. Enter the forty-one-year-old **Queen Victoria** *followed by* **Prince Albert**, *who is indeed terminally ill.*

Queen Well, Mr Boucicault – we have seen your play three times now, and we have enjoyed it as much as ever.

Boucicault Indeed, ma'am, we are thrice blessed.

Queen You show us our Irish subjects in the manner that renders them the most beloved to us.

Boucicault *addresses* **Prince Albert** *in* **Myles-Na-Coppaleen**'s *voice.*

Boucicault Ach, sir, it's a shamrock itself ye have got; and like that flower she'll come up every year fresh and green fornent ye. When ye cease to love her may dying become ye, and when you do die, leave your money to the poor, your widow to me, and we'll both forgive ye.

A shocked silence; defused by the **Queen**.

Queen Oh, wait, I believe I can recall it . . . (*Taking* **Eily**'s *lines from the play*.) I'm only a poor simple girl, and it's frightened I am to be surrounded by so many . . .

Hardress   Friends, Eily, friends . . . er, your
majesty . . .

Queen   Oh, if I could think so – if I could hope that I
had established myself in a little corner of their hearts,
there wouldn't be a happier girl alive than the Colleen
Bawn!

Boucicault, Agnes *and* **Hardress** *applaud.* **Prince
Albert** *steps aside a little, mopping his brow. He sways
unsteadily and reaches out an arm, which* **Boucicault** *catches.*

Queen   Albert, dearest . . .

Albert   Nothing at all, don't worry, I am not used to
such bright lights.

Boucicault (Myles *again*)   Sure, it's only heavy you
are, sir, like my own hogshead of poteen there – but
you only want tapping for pure spirits to flow out
spontaneously, perhaps.

Albert   Perhaps, yes, it is known as the water of life
after all, is it not?

Queen   Allow us to congratulate you all once more,
and to wish you continued success.

And she exits, looking anxiously at **Albert,** *who wearily follows
her off.* **Patterson** *ushers* **Hardress** *off behind them, and
then resumes his footman post.* **Boucicault** *meanwhile is
removing his* **Myles-Na-Coppaleen** *outfit.*

Agnes   Dion – you make far too free with her, playing
the fool like that.

Boucicault   I am her fool. I have the royal licence.

Agnes   You were playing the Vampire the last time
she praised you, but it didn't mean you could sink your
teeth in her neck.

Boucicault   Myles-na-Coppaleen has stronger teeth

than any vampire, Agnes. This age has made a mockery
of all my aspirations ... at long last I realise that
mockery is my own best friend. No limits to what it can
achieve, judiciously applied. We are clearly going to be
playing this piece for some considerable time.

Agnes   I never dreamt we would ever return home to
such acclaim!

Boucicault   I bought a house today, by the way.

Agnes   We don't need a house here, Dion, we already
own two houses in New York.

Boucicault   England denied my star its rightful
ascendancy ... I have returned to London for one
reason only, to claim my just inheritance by force.

Agnes   Where is it?

Boucicault   The Brompton Road, it's one of a pair of
mansions. I bought the other one as well, actually, but
purely as an investment, shall we dance?

Waltz music. **Boucicault** *sweeps* **Agnes** *into the dance, as a
glittering candelabra appears above their heads.* **Benjamin
Webster** *enters.*

Patterson   Mr Benjamin Webster!

The music stops.

Agnes   Mr Webster!

Webster   My dear Agnes.

Agnes   Do please excuse me, I really must go and
change.

Webster   Of course.

Agnes *exits.*

Webster   As for you, Dion, you never really change,
do you?

Boucicault   All the time, Benjamin. At the behest of the age, I constantly seek to improve myself.

Webster   Entirely at the expense of others.

Boucicault   How else?

Webster   Specifically at the expense of me.

Boucicault   Market forces, Benjamin. Personally, I subscribe to the Free Trade League.

Webster   You dare patronise me . . .

Boucicault   Do I? It's more than you ever did for me, patronage was a thing of the past, according to you – the artist must make his own way, on the open market, very well, I'm making a killing my own way, Webster, congratulate me.

Webster   The Adelphi Theatre is still mine! You have no right to make me a stranger in my own house – you already control the entire creative enterprise, you get half my profits, plus your existing fees, and now to cap it all, these damned royalty payments!

Boucicault   In return for which you are guaranteed capacity houses for *The Colleen Bawn* into the foreseeable future.

Webster   On the assumption that you even bother to honour our agreement.

Boucicault   But Benjamin – you and I are men of honour.

Charles Matthews *and* **Madame Vestris** *enter.*

Patterson   Mr Charles Matthews and Madame Vestris!

Waltz music. **Boucicault** *dances with* **Vestris.** **Charles Matthews** *and* **Benjamin Webster** *stroll off together. The music stops.*

Vestris   Your new house is a monument to your taste

and accomplishments, Dion.

Boucicault   Madame is kind.

Vestris   And I gather that you are building a theatre to match?

Boucicault   That will come in due course. Meanwhile, I have taken a lease on Astley's Amphitheatre.

Vestris   Astley's? You are surely not forsaking us for the circus?

Patterson *sniggers.* **Boucicault** *shoots him a look.*

Boucicault   I am converting the building into a legitimate theatre.

Vestris   What a charming idea. A theatre in the middle of Lambeth Marsh!

Patterson   Mrs Anne Boursiquot!

Waltz music. **Vestris** *sweeps off as* **Boucicault** *greets his mother and leads her into the dance. The music stops abruptly.*

Anne   An overgrown headstrong schoolboy, who has yet to learn the meaning of manhood.

Boucicault   What would you know about that, you surrendered your will into the power of a spider and a swindler.

Anne   I loved a man, it is love itself that you are incapable of!

Boucicault   You made yourself a slave, I will not live like that, Mother – I am going to be master of my own fate, however hard they try to ensnare and cage me!

Anne   Poor Mr Webster turned his whole theatre over to you – and all the thanks he gets is to be dragged through the courts of law. It's time you remembered your place.

Boucicault   My place is in history and posterity, those

are the only gods I acknowledge, and neither of them
will give a tinker's curse for Mr Webster.

Anne   The one and only god you know is money –
and you're throwing it to the four winds regardless.

Boucicault   I am in the process of creating a great
new London playhouse – the Theatre Royal,
Westminster.

Anne   Even I know it's not in Westminster, Dion – it's
on Lambeth Marsh.

Boucicault   It is a matter of yards across the river.

Anne   You can maybe adapt other people's plays – but
even you cannot rewrite the geography of London!

And she flounces out.

Patterson   Mr and Mrs George Jordan!

Waltz music. **Emily Jordan**, *a young actress in*
Boucicault's *company, enters with her husband* **George**.
Boucicault *sweeps her tempestuously into the dance.* **George**
Jordan *watches them for a bit, stiff with suspicion. Then he
turns on his heel and strides off. The candelabra disappears from
view, whilst two freestanding apartment doors as in a mansion
block of flats, are positioned upstage by* **Patterson.**
Boucicault *and* **Emily Jordan** *continue waltzing together as
the lights dim. When the music stops, they kiss.*

Emily   You took so long.

Boucicault   Espionage.

Emily   George has always suspected his own shadow.

Boucicault   There is a way to get rid of shadows.
Extinguish all the lights.

Emily   But Dion . . . we shall be entirely in the dark.

Boucicault   So will he, with any luck.

They disappear through the right-hand door. After a moment, loud *knocking is heard from off. The landlady – **Mrs Bechstein** – appears, and crosses towards the noise.*

Mrs Bechstein   We have ears, we come, please to leave a little paint on the door . . .

*She is off. The right-hand door re-opens, and the heads of **Emily Jordan** and **Boucicault** pop nervously out.*

Emily   Oh my God, he has tracked us down.

Boucicault   I will not be condemned to inhabit a farce!

Patterson   It's a bit late in the day to be saying that.

Emily   Dion, quickly, where can you hide?

Patterson   You mean you have no piano?

Boucicault *goes calmly to the left-hand door, tries it – it opens.*

Boucicault   Whose apartment is this?

Emily   Colonel Gibbon's.

Boucicault   Au revoir. (*And he disappears through the door.*)

Emily   Dion! Ah!

*The altercation from offstage is reaching a peak. **Emily** slips back in behind her own door just as her husband strides onstage, with **Mrs Bechstein** in his wake.*

Jordan   Which is her door, woman?

Mrs Bechstein   Please to wait in lobby pending announcement.

Jordan *hammers on the left-hand door.*

Jordan   Emily!

Mrs Bechstein *gives a genteel tap on **Emily**'s door.*

Mrs Bechstein   Please to remember you are now in Mayfair and try to act like gentleman.

Emily *opens her door.*

Emily   Why, Mrs Bechstein, what on earth is all the commotion . . . ? (*Seeing* **Jordan**.) So it is you. Leave here at once.

Jordan   Bring him out here. (*Shouting past her.*) Boucicault!

Emily   Nothing further remains to be said between us, George . . .

And she makes to close the door, but he forces it open, thrusts her aside and storms on in.

   . . . aah! Mrs Bechstein – this ruffian is a violent former husband of mine, kindly summon the constabulary.

Mrs Bechstein   Police? I do not like, in my house.

Emily   I see, you would much prefer a murder enquiry . . .

Mrs Bechstein   I go.

As **Mrs Bechstein** *hurries off she passes* **Colonel Gibbon** *– in his full ceremonials – entering.*

Gibbon   Evening, Mrs Bluthner.

He approaches his front door.

Emily (*leaping to intercept him*)   Colonel Gibbon!

Gibbon   Madam . . . don't believe I've had the um . . .

Emily   Emily Thorne. Miss. I'm your new neighbour, Colonel.

Gibbon   I say. How'd do.

Emily   Tell me . . . how is your regiment keeping? These days?

Gibbon (*at a loss*)   Well now . . . by Jove . . .

Jordan *bursts back through* **Emily**'s *door.*

Jordan   He will not elude me, I saw him enter this whorehouse with my bare eyes, bring the despicable kite before me!

Emily (*drawing the* **Colonel** *aside*)   An intruder in our midst, Colonel, never mind, a constable has been summoned . . .

Jordan's *eye falls on* **Colonel Gibbon**'s *door.*

Jordan   He is in there!

He tries to open the **Colonel**'s *door, but* **Boucicault** *has prudently locked it from the inside.*

Jordan   Who has the key?

Gibbon   Confound it, sir, that door is mine.

Jordan   Open it.

Gibbon (*to* **Emily**)   Are you acquainted with this fellow?

Jordan   There is a contemptible fugitive from the laws of God and man cowering behind that door, and I intend to bring him to justice!

Gibbon (*again to* **Emily**)   Is he a lunatic?

Emily   Yes I am and yes he is!

Gibbon (*turning to* **Jordan**)   Come along, my man. Be off with you.

Jordan   Are you going to unlock that door?

Gibbon   You heard me. Remove yourself from this house. (**Jordan** *grabs him by the throat.*)

Jordan (*shaking him*)   GIVE – ME – THE – KEY!

Music, to which the ensuing routine is choreographed. **Emily** *screams as the two men grapple with each other and stagger back and forth.* **Jordan** *succeeds in toppling* **Colonel Gibbon** *to the ground.* **Mrs Bechstein** *re-enters with* **Patterson** –

wearing a police constable's helmet – in tow. He hauls **Jordan**
off the **Colonel***, who is helped up and dusted down by* **Emily**
and the landlady. While they are all thus diverted,
Boucicault *slips out from behind the* **Colonel***'s door and*
back in through **Emily***'s unnoticed.* **Jordan** *expostulates with*
the **Constable** (**Patterson**)*, stating his case, the*
Constable *tries* **Colonel Gibbon***'s door – which now of*
course opens – and leads the rest of them through it, to check out
Jordan*'s accusations.* **Boucicault** *re-emerges from behind*
Emily*'s door, and slips into the shadows in a downstage corner.*
The others pour out through the **Colonel***'s door again, and off –*
the **Constable** *frog-marching a protesting* **Jordan***,* **Emily**
flirtatiously arm-in-arm with a delighted **Colonel Gibbon***,*
and **Mrs Bechstein** *plodding along complainingly in the rear.*
Patterson *chucks* **Jordan** *into the wings and throws the police*
constable's helmet after him, then turns back towards
Boucicault *as the music ends.*

Patterson   Nicely played, Boosy. Shame it all had to
come out in court, though, wasn't it?

And he sets about removing the two apartment doors.

Boucicault   The whole thrupenny scandal was
deliberately trumped up in order to discredit my name.

Patterson   No easy task.

Boucicault   They ganged up, same as ever, to force
me out of the business. The men of honour, propriety
and decorum saw to it that my Theatre Royal in
Westminster was shunned.

Patterson   Oh, yeah – the circus ring down Lambeth
way, you mean?

Boucicault   I was declared bankrupt.

Patterson   Not again.

Boucicault   Dispossessed, my theatre and house sold
to the highest bidder, driven back out into the provinces
like an outlaw ... but I hadn't forgotten New York.

Badger and Bloodgood. If a sensation drama could draw a credulous rabble in one city, why not in another? If *The Poor of New York* – why not *The Poor of Liverpool?*

Patterson   Tomorrow Liverpool will ring from Williamson Square to the Pierhead with the news – Bloodgood has absconded . . .

Boucicault   If Liverpool, why not Leeds or Hull, or Glasgow? I sowed my dragon's teeth the length and breadth of Britain, every city clamouring in half-witted support of its own local sensation, *The Poor of Newcastle*, *The Poor of Bristol* . . . until the honourable ranks of the West End managers finally burst asunder, in a mad scramble for the rights. I re-did the wretched farrago one final time, as *The Streets of London* . . . they flocked to it in droves. The burning down of Badger's hovel had set the entire nation on fire!

Patterson   You know what it is, Boosy – you are a walking testimonial to those values which have made our Victorian Age a golden one – plunder, greed, hypocrisy, cynicism, pious self-righteousness . . .

Boucicault   I played the hand they dealt me, and the little power I earned from it was applied to the service of my own people!

Patterson   Yourself and your mother, you mean?

Boucicault   I have done far more in the Irish cause than ever you achieved, you footling little balladmonger, I wrote 'Arrah-na-Pogue', and I wrote 'The Wearing of the Green' to go with it, the very anthem of the National movement!

Patterson (*sings*)
    Oh, Paddy dear! an' did you hear
    The news that's going round?
    The shamrock is by law forbid
    To grow on Irish ground . . .

Boucicault I insisted that the world premiere of that play be given in Dublin!

Patterson (*sings*)
    St Patrick's Day no more we'll keep
    His colours can't be seen,
    For there's a cruel law agin
    The wearing of the green ...

Boucicault They cheered me through the streets after it, two other theatres were staging *The Colleen Bawn* simultaneously, as a tribute!

Patterson (*sings*)
    She's the most distressful country
    That ever yet was seen,
    For they're hanging men and women there
    For wearin' of the green.

(*Speaks.*) Sure that's an ould song that everybody knows, you learnt it from your ma.

Boucicault The tune I may have learnt, the words I wrote myself.

Patterson Re-wrote, you mean.

Boucicault They are my words!

Patterson You and your work have the one thing in common – dubious paternity.

Boucicault I gave benefits, all over the country, to raise money for the Fenian prisoners' families. There was a bomb went off outside Clerkenwell prison ...

Patterson Twelve dead, a hundred and twenty injured.

Boucicault I deplored it. Even so, after it happened, 'The Wearing of the Green' was forbidden to be sung anywhere in the British Empire.

Patterson You were thrilled to bits about that, weren't you? I'll tell you what it really is, Boosy – you

love to play the poacher – so long as you're still
officially the gamekeeper.

Boucicault   It was I who challenged Disraeli to release
the Fenian prisoners!

Patterson   Yeah – after you'd finalised arrangements
to become an American citizen. You heard what Dizzy
said when they showed him your letter? 'Boucicault?
Boucicault? Where have I heard that name before? Is it
someone in the conjuring business?'

Boucicault   He has had leisure since to regret his
condescension.

Patterson   Sure, what of it? Didn't you get your free
publicity?

Boucicault   It was no stunt! Many times I went to the
Houses of Parliament to consult with members of the
Irish Party. It was made very clear to me that should I
wish to volunteer my services, I could choose my own
constituency.

Patterson   By God, that would have turned the trick
all right – Conn the Shaughraun, at the dispatch box –
speaking in support of Charles Stewart Parnell! (*Doing*
Conn.) 'Long life to yer honours, and isn't it a grand
thing for a tatterdemalion the likes of my poor self to be
addressin' all you fine English gentlemen? I freely
confess I nivir did an honest day's work in my life
before this – but drinkin' and fishin' and shootin' and
sportin' and love-makin' – sure it's the House of Lords I
belong in by rights! Beggin' your pardons . . .'

Boucicault   I can understand your bitterness. The
same people who slaughtered you showered me with
honours.

Patterson   Sure, why wouldn't they? You flattered the
daylights out of them, with your silver-tongued charming
peasant rascals, and all their winning, wheedling,

conniving ways ... your colonial soul discovered its
strength in fraudulence and deceit, Dizzy had you right,
you were in the conjuring business, you conjured up a
never-never Emerald Island, fake heroics and mettlesome
beauties and villains made of pasteboard, outwitted
through eternity by the bogus grinning peasant rogue as
only you could play him – with the blather and
codology and the gaslight moonshine.

Boucicault   People need laughter and lyricism,
reassurance, why not? – a sweet dream to drive out the
nightmares – who the blazes are you to talk, you offered
them the same thing!

Patterson *slowly smiles.*

Patterson   There you are, now. You and me both.
Paddy the Clown. Will we call it a day?

Boucicault   NO!

He falls to his knees.

Patterson   Only a matter of time, old fella. You were
already fifty-five when you wrote *The Shaughraun*, don't
forget.

*He has fetched a tin of white powder from the make-up box, and
he stands behind the kneeling* **Boucicault** *and whitens his
remaining hair during the following.*

Patterson   That was your last real success, now, am I
right?

Boucicault   I have plays in me still.

Patterson   They're all agreed you've outlived your
time.

Boucicault   They're saying my mind has gone, that
I'm senile, any scurrilous damnable lie to try and force
me under for the last time, I won't submit. I have never
stopped writing.

Patterson   You don't think you've maybe penned enough of them plays by now? How many is it anyhow? Any advance on two hundred?

Boucicault   It's of no importance, only the work matters, I am no Conn the Shaughraun, I have worked every day of my life and most nights, work is the one thing that gives this life an illusion of meaning . . .

Patterson   Except for marriage, of course.

Boucicault *stiffens, clambers to his feet.*

Patterson   Agnes appeared in *The Shaughraun* with you, I take it?

Boucicault   For a spell, she did.

Agnes *enters, dressed as* **Moya** – *the simple peasant girl who is* **Conn***'s beloved in* The Shaughraun – *and carrying a bunch of wild flowers.*

Moya   Ah! Conn, do you see those flowers? I picked them by the wayside as I came along, and I put them in my breast. They are dead already. The life and fragrance have gone out of them. Killed by the heat of my heart. So it may be with you, since I picked you and put you there. Won't the life go out of your love? Hadn't I better leave you where you are?

Patterson   Twenty-five years of faithful marriage to you. Six children she gave you, and working throughout it all, playing every role you demanded of her, trailing after you all over the map.

Boucicault   She didn't go unrewarded.

Patterson   Watching you, truffling away under the skirt of every new young actress in the company, that was her reward, you mangy old goathead. Dionysius Lardner rides again.

Agnes   Dion . . .

Boucicault   All right! Enough! Go home, Agnes. It's over.

Agnes *tosses the flowers aside and pulls off the* **Moya** *shawl.*

Agnes   I no longer remember even which mistress it was ... one of the passing fancies, clearly, not one that you actually lived with, there were such a lot it's hard to recall it now ... you bought her a cottage in Kent, I think, and a rather hideous jardinière, made from streaky green marble, I remember the jardinière, you see, because for some extraordinary reason it was just then that it all finally died for me. So you needn't any longer fear that I am going to cling on and beg and plead for you to respect me as your wife, yet again ... I barely even remember what being loved by you felt like. However – we do still have children, Dion, and I do not consider it kind to them for their father to be living with other women three thousand miles away ... so. Since at least the geography is surmountable, I suggest that I bring them here to New York to live. Or else that you return to London.

Boucicault   You are free to run your own life, so will they be soon enough, kindly allow me to get on with mine.

Agnes   Free ... you're not free, never can be free, Dion. You've spent your whole career pitting yourself against the Age, fulminating against it ... when all the time the savagery of the Age was concentrated in you, every life you have ever touched has been a victim of it, sacrificed on the altar of your work ... but surely you know your plays will amount to little more than breaking wind in a stiff breeze, at the end of all, that your last and worst victim is you yourself, Dion? Because the truth is, you *are* the Age. It's all there is to you.

Boucicault   How much do you need?

Agnes   One thousand seven hundred and fifty dollars, for the moment.

Boucicault   Precise as ever.

Agnes   I have two of the girls with me, as you're well aware, it's the cost of transporting us all back to London.

Boucicault   Cheap at the price. Here, take it. (*Giving her the money.*)

Agnes   Thank you, Dion. I gather your new play is expected to flop, yet again. We'll be thinking of you.

She exits.

Patterson   The new flop in question being entitled – what else – *The Jilt!* In which Myles O'Hara, an ageing bohemian jockey and gentleman of the turf, arrives at The Abbots, the ancestral home of Sir Buddleigh Woodstock and his pretty young sister Kitty.

The backdrop parts, to reveal **Marcus Wylie**, *the villain, alone with* **Kitty Woodstock**, *the heroine.*

Wylie   Kitty – can I do nothing to please you?

Kitty   I will tell you what *not* to do, Sir Marcus. Don't follow me about with a box of sweets as children try to catch birds by putting a piece of salt on their tails. If ever I do fall in love, I must plunge into it unawares – and before I know where I am.

She is striding off and runs straight into the arms of **Boucicault**, *who has entered the scene in the character of* **Myles O'Hara**.

Kitty   Oh!

O'Hara   For what we have received, may the Lord make us truly thankful.

Kitty   I beg your pardon, sir. (*And she makes her way off.*)

Wylie   You present yourself without much ceremony.

O'Hara   Egad, sir, it was the most delightful ceremony I ever encountered. (*Offering card, which* **Wylie** *takes.*)

Wylie   Myles O'Hara? I beg your pardon. Your name is so celebrated that I feel we are already acquainted. I shall tell Sir Buddleigh of your arrival.

He exits.

Patterson   The part of Kitty Woodstock having been written for that vivacious young newcomer, Miss Louise Thorndyke, who will now afford us a foretaste of the thrilling denouement!

Louise Thorndyke – Kitty Woodstock *– re-enters, and addresses* **Boucicault**.

Kitty   Mr O'Hara, I cannot quite understand you. Do you know that you are the only man that has been received here who has never made love to me?

O'Hara   Good heavens, Miss Woodstock! What d'you take me for? Do you think I should mistake myself so far? You know who and what I am.

Kitty   I think so.

O'Hara   And who and what you are. Think of the extreme distance between us.

Kitty   Extremes meet sometimes.

O'Hara   I am a poor broken-down adventurer, penniless, homeless – a bohemian in the city, a vagabond in the shires, I am a tramp that stops at your gate, and takes a hungry look at you through the bars.

Kitty   So you are going to leave us?

O'Hara   And I leave my life here.

Kitty   In the stable with your horse?

O'Hara   No! at your feet. I can't help it. Your eyes wring it out of my soul. I must speak or die.

Kitty   Then speak for heaven's sake.

O'Hara   I may offend you.

Kitty   The only offence has been your silence.

O'Hara   My love . . .

Kitty   Yes, yours.

He kisses her.

Patterson   Pardon me for butting in, but what theatre is this exactly?

Boucicault   The Theatre Royal, Sydney.

Patterson   Sydney?

Boucicault   We took the play on a tour across Australia. It was in Sydney that Louise and I were married. (*Taking her hand.*)

Patterson   You mean . . . on top of everything else you've become a bigamist?

Boucicault   NO! (*To* **Louise**.) It's not so.

Louise *smiles at him, and exits.* **Boucicault** *steps downstage as the backdrop closes.*

Boucicault   The supposed marriage between Agnes Robertson and myself had never legally existed.

Patterson   So. You were ready and willing to reduce your wife to a harlot in the eyes of society, and to see your children illegitimised and disinherited – the very grievances you yourself have been whingeing about all morning?

Boucicault   There was none of that, it was all just words and pieces of paper!

Patterson   What else is your entire life?

Boucicault   I needed to marry Louise!

Patterson   You were sixty-five.

Boucicault   Sixty-four.

Patterson   She was twenty-one!

Boucicault   I had to start over again, cut all the strings, can't you understand? I had played by their rules, the whole time, I had to master my own fate, once and for all, in the teeth of all their hollow gods. I have a multitude of plays in me still!

Patterson   The judge found in favour of Agnes.

Boucicault   Made no odds, Louise and I had a second wedding, here in New York, after the divorce.

Patterson   What about the alimony?

Boucicault   How do they expect me to pay it, I have no money.

Patterson   All them flops.

Boucicault   I do a little teaching – here, in this theatre, the Madison Square, they have started a drama school, it keeps me in touch with the young people which is where I most belong ... I've just been somewhat tired lately, nothing serious, I think I may have caught something, it's been raining for days now ...

Patterson *is bringing on a brass bed.*

Boucicault   What are you doing?

Patterson   I'm putting you to bed, Boosy. You don't sound a bit well.

He leads **Boucicault** *to the bed and pulls back the covers.*

Patterson   Get tucked in there like a good man and I'll sing you a little lullaby.

Boucicault *gets into the bed, as* **Patterson** *sings quietly.*

Patterson (*singing*)
> I'm very happy where I am
> Far across the say,
> I'm very happy far from home
> In North Amerikay . . .

(*Speaks.*) This is one of your own devising, d'you mind it at all?

Boucicault   Why wouldn't I? It's more than a match for any of your come-all-ye's.

Patterson   Sure we're songbirds of a feather, the pair of us.

(*Sings.*)
> It's lonely in the night, when Pat
> Is sleeping by my side,
> I lie awake and no-one knows
> The big tears that I've cried . . .
> For a little voice still calls me back
> To my far, far countrie,
> And nobody can hear it spake,
> O, nobody but me . . .

(*Speaks.*) Calling you home, Boosy – but sure where is there a home for the likes of you? Apart from centre stage with the bright light on you?

(*Sings.*)
> There is a certain spot of ground
> lt makes a dawny hill,
> And from below the voice comes out,
> I cannot keep it still . . .

Boucicault (*starting up feverishly*)   NO! I will not go under!

Louise Thorndyke *comes running on.*

Louise   Dion, dearest, it's all right . . .

Boucicault   I am not yet ready to go!

Louise   There's no need, you're not well, they're not
expecting you to go.

Boucicault (*looking at her amazed*)   What are you talking
about?

Louise   The theatre school, of course.

Boucicault *gives vent to a harsh laugh.*

Louise   Your students have sent you crocuses and
lilies.

Boucicault   Have they indeed, kindly inform them
they're a little bit previous with their funeral tributes.

Louise   You know quite well they are very impatient
for your return.

Boucicault   Louise . . .

Louise   Yes, darling?

Boucicault   My play – *A Tale of a Coat* – bad news. It
closed at the weekend.

Louise   Hush, it's all right, I know all about that.

Boucicault   For eleven long years they have denied
me a success . . . I have written for a monster who
forgets.

Louise   You are the greatest man of the theatre in this
age, every passer-by in the street knows that.

Boucicault *slips out of bed and addresses the house.*

Boucicault   She says you will go bail for me . . . you
are the only friend I have. Long life t'ye! – Many a
time have you looked over my faults – will you be blind
to them now and hould out your hands once more to a
poor Shaughraun?

Louise   Dion, please come back to bed.

Boucicault   You know, when I wrote that kind of
speech, the older actors were scandalised by it. They
were accustomed to exit lines, you see, without them

they felt simply stranded on the stage. They used to say to me, 'Dear boy, can't you possibly offer me a few words to take me off, you've left me high and dry ...' You see the foolishness of it, Louise, they literally couldn't get off, couldn't leave the stage, just a few words, all that's needed, those precious few, so long as they're the right ones, to turn the trick, the exact few words that'll manage at last please God to GET ME OFF!

He collapses. She rushes over, helps him up and back to the bed.

Louise   Don't, don't, come on now, I'm putting you back to bed ... help me, Dion ... come along, that's it, you're going to get well ... (*She has manhandled him into bed.*) Darling, I'm going to fetch the doctor now, please just lie quiet until I get back, all right?

She kisses him, walks to the side of the stage.

I shall only be gone for a moment. (*She exits.*)

Patterson   She had the words to get her off, did you notice?

He stands at the head of the bed looking down at **Boucicault**, *and resumes singing the song.*

O, little voice, ye call me back
To my far, far countrie,
And nobody can hear ye speak,
O, nobody but me ...

(*Speaks.*) You've had your day in court now, Boosy. You're being sent down.

Boucicault   Could we not at least do the wake before we go?

Patterson   You're not getting any wake. You're too high-falutin' now for that class of a send-off.

Boucicault   Not mine, not my wake – Conn's.

Patterson   Eh?

Boucicault   From *The Shaughraun*. The Wake Scene.

Patterson   Ah, merciful Jaysus, not another scene from a play . . .

Boucicault   All the accoutrements are in place, it won't detain you more than a minute. It was the finest scene of my career.

Patterson   Weren't they all?

Boucicault   The audience knows that Conn is actually alive – but his mother and the neighbours take him for dead, you see . . .

Patterson   I know the gag, just start the bloody music.

Music: 'The Oolaghaun'. **Mrs O'Kelly, Conn**'s *grieving widowed mother, is helped on by two male mourners. They are followed by the chief keener,* **Biddy Madigan**. *All of them are carrying bottles and jugs of liquor, and lighted candles, and they are singing the lament for the dead.*

All

Och, Oolaghaun! – och Oolaghaun!
Make his bed both wide and deep!
Och, Oolaghaun! – och Oolaghaun!
He is only gone to sleep.
Why did ye die? – oh, why did ye die?
And lave us all alone to cry?

Biddy (*wailing*)   Oh, oh, oho! (*Rocking herself.*) The widow had a son – an only son – wail for the widow!

All (*singing*)

Why did ye die? – Why did ye die?

They have grouped themselves around the bed: **Boucicault** *is once again* **Conn the Shaughraun**.

Biddy   The boy grew strong, for she fed him with her heart's blood. A, hogoola! Where is he now? Cowld in his bed! Why did ye die?

All (*singing*)
  Leaving us to sigh! Och, hone!

Biddy   None was like him – none could compare . . .
(*Breaking off: an aside to the nearest mourner, **Sullivan**.*) . . .
good luck to ye, gimme a drop of somethin' to put the
spirit in one, for the fire's gettin' low.

Sullivan *hands her a jug of punch.*

Mrs O'Kelly   It's mighty consolin' to hear this . . . Mr
Malone, you are not eatin'.

Mourner   No, ma'am, I'm drinkin'. I drink now and
again, by way of variety. (*Aside to **Sullivan**.*) Biddy is not
up to herself.

Sullivan   Oh, wait till she'll rise on the top of that
noggin.

Biddy *has taken a long draught. She now places the jug by the
bed and rises again to the occasion.*

Biddy   He was brave! He was brave! He had the heart
of a lion and the legs of a fox.

Conn *picks up the jug, drains it dry, and replaces it, unobserved
by the other characters.*

Biddy   His voice was softer than the cuckoo of an
evening, and sweeter than the blackbird after a summer
shower. Ye colleens, ye will never hear the voice of
Conn again! (*She blows her nose.*)

Conn (*to the house*)   It's a mighty pleasant thing to die
like this, once in a way, and hear all the good things
said about ye after ye're dead and gone, when they can
do you no good.

Biddy   His name will be the pride of the O'Kellys for
evermore!

Conn   I was a big blackguard when I was alive.

Biddy   Noble and beautiful!

Conn   Ah, go on out o' that!

Biddy (*picking up her jug*)   Oh, he was sweet and strong
. . . who the divil's been at my jug of punch?

Mrs O'Kelly   Nobody is drinkin' – yez all despise the
occasion!

Knocking from without.

Sullivan   What's that?

Enter **Captain Molineux**, *the hapless young English officer
in the play.*

Molineux   I don't come to disturb this . . . a . . .
melancholy . . . a . . . entertainment . . . I mean, a . . .
this festive solemnity . . .

Mrs O'Kelly   Heaven bless you for coming to admire
the last of him. Here he is – isn't he beautiful?

Molineux (*aside*)   The vagabond is winking at me.

Mrs O'Kelly   How often have I put him to bed as a
child, and sung him to sleep! Now he will be put to bed
with a shovel, and oh! the song was never sung that will
awaken him.

Molineux   If any words could put life into him, I
came here to speak them. A reprieve has been granted!
A heavenly abode is prepared for him in spite of all!

A moment's silence, then they all burst out cheering and carry
Molineux *off on their shoulders.*

Boucicault (*sitting up*)   I never wrote that. What did he
mean?

Patterson   I assume you're still hell-bent on being
counted amongst the angels?

Boucicault   Appeal dismissed was the verdict, as I
understood it.

Patterson   Ah, I'm prepared to stretch a point. It was
a tidy little scene all right, that wake, I'll grant you that.

Boucicault   I could show you more, if you like . . .

Patterson (*hastily*)   Another time, maybe, we have to see about getting you upstairs. You're being buried from the Church of the Transfiguration, what do you think of that, now?

Boucicault   Will there be a decent turnout?

Patterson   Not bad, for a matinee. Are you ready?

Boucicault   Ready.

Patterson   Good luck, then, Boosy, no hard feelings, nice knowing you.

Patterson *retires with funeral gravity to the side. Organ music.* **Boucicault** *settles himself in dignified repose. The backdrop parts to reveal twinkling heavens, with a great central star bearing* **Boucicault***'s portrait. The members of the company enter in mourning dress, and lay wreaths and flowers all over the bed. The bed begins to ascend to heaven. The mourners doff their hats and fall to their knees. A heavenly choir is heard. Music and singing build towards a climax, as the levitating* **Boucicault** *climbs ever more heavenwards, and his star lights up and sparkles. Suddenly water starts cascading down on the catafalque.* **Boucicault** *sits up smartly – he is getting drenched. The music and the heavenly choir stop abruptly.*

Patterson   Ah, holy God, isn't that just typical? The heavens open, and what happens? – the rain comes through the bloody roof!

The star and all the other lights flash, crackle, fuse and expire. Circus music. Blackout.

Pentecost

Pentecost was first performed at the Guildhall, Derry, by the Field Day Theatre Company on 23 September 1987 with the following cast:

Lenny   Stephen Rea
Marian   Eileen Pollock
Lily   Barbara Adair
Ruth   Paula Hamilton
Peter   Jonathan Kent

Directed by Patrick Mason
Designed by Bunny Christie
Lighting by Conleth White

The English premiere was presented by the Tricycle Theatre Company at the Lyric Theatre, Hammersmith, on 9 January 1989 with the following cast:

Lenny   Adrian Dunbar
Marian   Dearbhla Molloy
Lily   Barbara Adair
Ruth   Michelle Fairley
Peter   Sam Dale

Directed by Nicholas Kent
Designed by Poppy Mitchell
Lighting by David Colmer

Act One

The time is 1974. The place is Belfast. The play takes place in the downstairs back part of a respectable working-class 'parlour' house, built in the early years of this century. There is a kitchen with a fireplace, a rocking-chair, a sofa, a dining table. On one side a doorway leads into the scullery, with its flagstone floor and its old cast-iron range for cooking on and its 'jawbox' of a sink. At the far end of the scullery another door leads into the pantry, which we can't see. The large kitchen window looks out on the back yard, which is very narrow, with high, whitewashed walls topped by lines of broken glass. The yard door is heavily bolted, even though its worn ribs are showing through.

On the other side of the kitchen is the door leading into the hall and thence to the rest of the house. There is an under-stairs cupboard by this door. There is a single electric light with conical shade hanging from the middle of the ceiling in kitchen and scullery both; but there are also working gas mantles on the walls. Everything is real except the proportions. The rooms are narrow, but the walls climb up and disappear into the shadows above the stage. The kitchen in particular is cluttered, almost suffocated, with the furnishings and bric-à-brac of the first half of the century, all the original fixtures and fittings still being in place. But in spite of now being shabby, musty, threadbare, it has all clearly been the object of a desperate, lifelong struggle for cleanliness, tidiness, orderliness — godliness.

The people are **Marian**, **Lenny** *and* **Peter**, *who are all thirty-three;* **Ruth**, *who is twenty-nine; and* **Lily Matthews**, *who is seventy-four.*

Scene One

A night in February. **Lenny** *is seated on the kitchen sofa, playing 'I Can't Get Started' on his trombone. His tape machine is on the* *table, providing the rhythm-section backing. He is wearing his overcoat and hat: it's very cold, there is no fire in the grate. Only the single electric lights are on.* **Marian** *enters from the hall, also in her overcoat. She switches off* **Lenny***'s backing track. His trombone peters out.*

Marian   Did you make tea?

Lenny   The gas is off.

Marian *has moved on into the kitchen, and is peering into a teapot on the top of the range.*

Marian   What's this?

Lenny   That's old. So. What do you reckon?

Marian   There's a cup sitting here with milk and sugar in it. Christ.

Lenny   I told you. I haven't touched a thing.

Marian   She must have brewed this up just before it happened.

Lenny   No such thing.

Marian   She never got a chance to pour it out.

Lenny   The ambulancemen, is all it would have been.

Marian   It's stone cold.

Lenny   The ambulancemen at the door, is all it possibly could have been.

Marian *turns her full attention on him for the first time.*

Marian   I see. They prepared a nice pot of tea, prior to removing the corpse.

Lenny   She walked out of here, in her Sunday hat and coat and best handbag, is what I'm saying, under her own steam, into the ambulance, it was in the hospital she died . . .

Marian   When?

Lenny   How do I know, under the anaesthetic.

Marian   When?

Lenny   Why?

Marian   I'm asking you when.

Lenny   What does it matter, Wednesday sometime . . .

Marian   Christ.

Lenny   Meaning what?

Marian   Why is her family not here?

Lenny   No surviving relatives, I told you. There wasn't even anybody at the funeral.

Marian   So. I wonder how they manage in a case like that.

Lenny   My Great-Aunt Rosaleen owned the whole terrace, it was all in her will, I told . . .

Marian   Holding a funeral when there's nobody at it, I mean.

Lenny   Very good, Marian. Right, well, let's see. The wee butcher from the shop on the front of the road was there, her churchgoing cronies, a few oul' dolls who used to live next door when there used to be a door next door, no family is actually of course what I was saying, okay? Me, I was there. Standing foundered in Dundonald at half nine this morning, being tonguelashed by the Free Presbyterian notion of a requiem mass, that was it. Just what *is* this?

Marian   You haven't exactly let the grass grow.

Lenny   Just how is this, whenever I start the evening doing you a favour, ten minutes into it and suddenly I'm a heartless creep, dishonouring the dead, I never once clapped eyes on the woman!

Marian   Well you've sure as hell inherited the woman.

Lenny The house, I've inherited the house, by law it has to come to me once the sitting tenant's dead, you think I ever wanted this? – I thought you'd maybe appreciate the chance, before there's any sort of an auction, you could have the pick of all this for your shop, you were never off my back about being careless with money, okay, great stuff, go ahead and take advantage of it.

Marian You haven't lost your knack of feeling put-upon, I see.

Lenny (*leaping up*) Forget I ever mentioned it, Marian.

Marian Sit down. Here. Stick this in your gub. (*Producing a half bottle of brandy from her shoulder-bag.*) What was her name?

Lenny Matthews. Mrs Alfred George Matthews.

Marian (*a toast*) God love you, Mrs Matthews.

Lenny Lily to her friends.

Marian Nice house, Lily, you kept it lovely.

She swigs and passes the bottle to **Lenny**, *who finally decides to accept it.*

Lenny Responsibilities, who needs them.

Marian Property used to be theft, in your book.

Lenny What are you supposed to do? It was my mother insisted I go to the funeral. 'That wee woman lived her whole life in that house, it's your responsibility now, the least you can do is honour her memory' – what memory? None of us even once met her. If she'd known her rent was going straight to the Legion of Mary, she'd have dropped dead years ago. The last thing she'd ever have asked for was me mooching round her graveside, did it never strike you that funerals and weddings are much of a muchness in this country?

Marian   Certainly. Our wedding was exactly like a funeral.

Lenny   There's just one way to tell the difference. Nobody takes photographs at a funeral.

Marian   Apart from the Special Branch.

She has wandered back into the kitchen and is examining a row of mugs displayed on a shelf.

Look at this. Queen Victoria's Diamond Jubilee, the wedding of Queen Mary, the Coronation of Lizzie the Second, 1953 – that must be the most modern item in the house. Most of the furniture's Edwardian, there's a Regency dressing table upstairs that must have come down through her grandparents.

Lenny   Is it all worth much? What do you reckon?

Marian *deliberates, moving about amongst the furniture.*

Marian   As I remember it – what was the word you most detested in the whole of the English language – 'antiques'.

Lenny   Yeah. Well. You felt much the same way about 'trombone'.

Marian   I didn't feel that different about 'antiques' as a matter of fact.

Lenny   Antiques have been your whole livelihood.

Marian   It's been my trade, I don't have to love it.

Lenny   You always loved it.

Marian   Things, individually crafted, well-cared-for, those I love, not the business, you never could grasp that. Old and beautiful things.

Lenny   The sash my father wore.

Marian   Up yours too. I've sold the shop. If you want to know.

Lenny *is thunderstruck.*

Lenny   You've done what?

Marian   For an amazingly good price, when you consider the state the city's in, but then it's what I'm good at, isn't it, as you're at pains to point out, trading, buying and selling. I don't have to love it. Just get on with it. Survival. It's one bloody useful knack, knowing the value of things to people, what they'll pay, what they think they're worth. The things, that is. The people of course are not worth shit. I didn't have to love them either. You and I tend to diverge on that point, you having all that deep-seated compassion, for anything that snuffles into your shoulder . . .

Lenny   Hold on a minute!

Marian   In my case the embattled bourgeoisie of Belfast was one long procession of avaricious gobshites – hell-bent on overloading their lounge cabinets and their display units with any bauble or knick-knack, so long as it looked like it cost more than it did, so long as it was showy enough to advertise their grandeur, and their fashionable taste and stylishness, not to mention their absolutely bottomless vulgarity, it was bad enough before the shooting-match started, it's grotesque at this point, I couldn't handle any more of it.

Lenny   Why Marian did it not maybe, I mean how come you never . . . ?

Marian   Besides I didn't have you to feed and clothe any more, so who needs it? Do you ever actually earn money these days?

Lenny   What do you imagine you're going to do?

Marian   You can't possibly get paid for playing that thing.

Lenny   Why did you bother coming here to look at this at all?

Marian   I need a house.

Lenny   You what? What do you mean, a house?
You're not thinking of starting up as an estate agent?

Marian   I need a house. To live in.

Lenny   You've got a flat to live in.

Marian   I've put it on the market.

Lenny   Marian ... Exactly what's going on with you?

Marian   Have you had this place valued?

Lenny   Of course I haven't had it bloody valued, the
woman was only buried this morning!

Marian   I'll buy it from you. Wholesale. House and
contents, just the way they stand at the minute. The
lock, the stock and the barrel. I'll pay you the going
price. Whatever the valuation is. We can go and see
your solicitor uncle first thing in the morning.

In the time that it takes for **Lenny** *to get to grips with this
bizarre notion, the soft booming of two distant explosions is heard.*

Lenny   What kind of game are we playing here?

Marian   Trading, buying and selling. The one I'm so
good at.

Lenny   God. The years I've spent wondering what
you'd hit me with next ...

Marian   I want the house. No joke.

Lenny   Talk sense!

Marian   You haven't lost your belief in the free spirit,
surely, the unencumbered impulse. The pure
spontaneous gesture. All that life-embracing bollocks that
I so conspicuously lacked, well here's me right now
acting like mad on impulse, Lenny, free-spirited as all
get out, so what exactly are we waiting for?

Lenny The name of the game, for a start.

Marian Who cares, imagine whatever takes your fancy, maybe I've noticed a Gainsborough lying behind the mangle, check it out. So long as we have a deal.

Lenny A deal, Marian – is what we don't actually have. You and me.

Marian Don't start that.

Lenny Still don't have, not since a year ago last May.

Marian Business is all I'm here to talk . . .

Lenny So fine, you want to buy this hovel for reasons as yet unexplained, that can certainly be arranged – providing we're agreeing to a brand new deal. Namely: The house is yours as stated, terms agreed. In return for a divorce.

Marian We are divorced, as good as.

Lenny I'm talking about your signature on a petition.

Marian What difference does it make?

Lenny It makes it official, it makes it binding, it makes it definite.

Marian Not in the one and only place where it actually means something . . .

Lenny The church? – the church is beneath my notice, it's beneath contempt, if the church won't recognise my divorce, that's fine, great. Because I don't recognise its existence. Because out here in the real world, Marian, we've been conducting separate lives in separate houses for one year ten months, where's the point, it's only suspended animation, I can't keep on like this, let's pull the plug and have done with it. I can't see what your difficulty is. (*She is silent.*) There's nobody else I'm planning to marry, if that's what you're thinking. There's nobody else full stop. It's got nothing to do with anybody else. (*She remains silent.*) We have no children, we have no mortgage, there's no argument over an estate, you were the one who made all the money anyway, you've got it all, what's your problem? What are you holding out for? We're never going to get together again, not in a million years, you can't stand me, less than ever, why prolong it? Let's get shot of it. What's your objection?

Marian *remains silent for a moment longer, then turns abruptly towards him.*

Marian Okay. Tomorrow morning. Your uncle can take care of that along with the house.

Lenny *is gobsmacked.*

Lenny Well. I'd rather it wasn't actually my Uncle Phelim. I mean, I don't mind, if you want to talk about it . . .

Marian You've said all there is. I agree.

Lenny I mean, I'm not trying to force you into a corner. It's something we need to feel the same way about.

Marian It's settled. We're doing it.

Lenny Ach, for Jesus' sake come off it, Marian, you can't possibly live in this gaff, it's the last house on the road left inhabited! – the very road itself is scheduled to vanish off the map, it's the middle of a redevelopment zone, not to mention the minor detail that it's slap bang in the firing line, the Prods are all up in that estate, (*Gesturing towards the back of the house.*) the Taigs are right in front of us, anyway look at it – it's reeking of damp, there's five different layers of wallpaper hanging off the walls, she was still using gas lamps in half the rooms, nothing to cook on apart from that ancient range, brown lino everywhere and rooms bunged up with junk, there's probably rats, mice and badgers in the belfry, it's riddled with rot and it's dingy, dank and absolutely freezing!

Marian   Perfect. I'll take it.

She sweeps out into the hall to take another look around. **Lenny** *is left staring after her, entirely at a loss for further words. He punches his cassette player on the table and the backing track is heard again. He picks up his trombone and plays along to it. The lights fade slowly to blackout.*

Scene Two

A night in April. The gaslight comes up on **Marian** *standing in the scullery, making herself a cup of coffee. She is wearing a sweater and skirt. She has lit the kitchen fire as well as the gas mantles. She carries her coffee into the kitchen and pauses to take a sip of it, gazing into the fire, the flames glimmering over her face. She sets the coffee down on the table, fetches the half bottle of brandy from her shoulder bag and unscrews the top.*

Marian   Begging your pardon, Lily Matthews. I'm sure no sup ever passed your lips. Show a little mercy. Some of us are made of weaker stuff.

She pours a shot of brandy into the coffee, and then carries both over to the rocking-chair, sits herself down and rocks a little.

Pleased to make your acquaintance, by the way. (*Holding up the coffee and taking a swig, as in a mock toast, and then setting down the coffee on the floor – which causes her to notice a raffia basket tucked in beside the chair. She picks it up, takes the lid off, lifts out a piece of unfinished knitting still on the needles.*) So. What was this going to be? (*She finds the pattern in the basket.*) Aha. A woolly bedjacket – by God you certainly need one in that bedroom. I might just finish it off for you. If you're sure you don't object to me wearing it, that is.

She rocks a little more.

I've got to make some plans for you and me, Lily
Matthews.

A low distant rumble of explosions is heard. **Lily Matthews**,
*in Sunday coat and hat and best handbag appears in the shadowy
doorway leading from the pantry.*

Lily   I don't want you in my house.

Marian *keeps her eyes on the knitting pattern: on guard but not
entirely frightened, aware that her mind is playing tricks on her.*

Marian   You needn't try to scare me, Lily.

Lily   Don't you 'Lily' me. I don't want you in here,
breathing strong drink and profanity, and your husband
deserted.

Marian   Maybe you'd prefer him.

Lily   I want no truck with any of yous, stay you with
your own and let me rest easy with mine.

Marian   Take a look – your things are in safe hands.

Lily   The hands of an idolater!

Marian   I've changed nothing. I've brought nothing
with me. See? No Sacred Hearts, no holy water, not
even a statue of yer woman – everything still in its place
the way you left it, the way you wanted it.

Lily   You're here. With all that's in you. (*Entering the
kitchen.*) This house was my life.

Marian   I know it was.

Lily   You know nothing about it. You'd be singing on
the other side of your face if my Alfie was here.

Marian (*closing her eyes*)   There's nobody here. Nobody.

Lily   It was Alfie Matthews found this house, it was
him that first put down the deposit, moved the pair of
us into it within a week of them building it – the year
of nineteen and eighteen – and me a bride at eighteen
years of age . . . Alfie had come back, that's why. Back

from Passchendaele. Hellfire Corner. Back from the
dead. Him and Jackie Midgely, the only two from Hope
Street, out of the twelve that went. All in the one week,
married and moved in, he wouldn't wait . . . not after
what he'd seen . . . this house was his life, same as mine.
He never left it, not for a night. Except the once, to try
and find work, in the Depression. That and the day
they carried him to his grave. You have no right to be
in here.

Marian (*raising the brandy*)   Alfie Matthews, God rest
him. (*Swigs.*) No doubt he was fond of a drop himself.

Lily   My man would take a stout like any other, of a
Friday night, what harm in that? He never lifted his
hand to me, not once, in forty-one years of marriage, no
matter what amount of drink was on him.

Marian   Must have died in '59, then.

Lily   He never harmed a living soul . . .

Marian   Fifteen years left on your own.

Lily   Every pipe in this house was laid by his hands,
the plumbing, the gas, gas fitting was his trade, every
pipe had to be put back and it was him put them back
. . . after your crowd burnt it down round us.

Marian   I don't want to hear this.

Lily   Three years we'd been in this street.

Marian   No end to reprisals, is there . . .

Lily   Three years of sacrificing for every little stick we
possessed, all that we'd managed to scrape together,
destroyed in the one night, it's a mercy we even lived
through it, me crouched in there, in that pantry, crying
out for the Lord Jesus to deliver us, Alfie out in the
yard trying to block up the back door, but they come
over the wall and bate him senseless to the ground and
on into this very kitchen roaring and rampaging like the

cruel heathens they were, smashing through those gas mantles with their clubs and cudgels till the whole house went up. I was trapped in that pantry for a solid hour. (*She moves back towards the pantry door.*) Alfie lying bleeding in the yard, if it hadn't been for the fire brigade lads moving in as fast as they did, I wouldn't be here now.

Marian   You're not here now.

Lily   Smoke and ashes, scorched walls, water flooded everywhere . . . my beautiful house . . . there was sky showing through a part of the rafters . . . every wee thing we'd saved up for ruined in the one night. By a pack of Fenian savages!

Marian   It was probably nothing personal, Lily.

Lily   Stay you away from where you're not welcome.

Marian   I have a problem with that, you see . . . seeing as the place where I'm least welcome of all is the inside of my own skull . . . so there's something we can agree on at least, Lily. I don't like me either.

From offstage comes the sound of urgent hammering at the front door. **Marian** *looks out into the hall, tense.*

Is this maybe a return bout – your mob calling round to take care of me? What do you think?

She turns her head back, but **Lily** *has melted away into the shadows of the pantry. The hammering is heard again.* **Marian** *moves out into the hall and calls.*

Marian   Who's there, please?

Ruth (*offstage*)   It's me, Marian. It's Ruth.

Marian   Ruth, is that you? Hang on a minute.

She exits, and we hear her opening the front door off.

(*Off.*) Come on in, what are you doing down here at this hour?

Ruth (*off*)   I wasn't sure of the house.

Marian   Go ahead.

We hear the front door being closed. **Ruth** *appears in the kitchen doorway, dressed in a long white raincoat, with a scarf wound tightly round her neck and a bandanna on her head, worn low over the eyes.*

Ruth   None of them seem to be working, the lamps. Out there.

Marian   They've stripped all the timers out of them, for the bombs.

Ruth   Yes. They do actually do that.

Marian   How did you track me down here, Ruth?

Ruth   I'm sorry, Marian.

Marian   I was only wondering.

Ruth   I suppose your idea is to sell all these old things.

Marian   Sit down.

Ruth   Nice big fire. (*She moves to it but doesn't sit down.*) It was just, earlier today, bumping into Lenny, are you really going to live down here, it's all a bit . . . all . . .

Marian   You need a drink?

Ruth   It's quite hard, getting here. That fire's quite warm. (*She yawns.*)

Marian   You might as well tell me about it, Ruth.

Ruth   I was just wondering, I know it's rather late to be asking, I would have phoned only you haven't got one, I did actually phone, at the flat, and the shop, not knowing, but anyway – if there was any chance, you could maybe put me up for the night, Marian.

Marian   What has he done to you this time?

Ruth *moves around, looking evasively out into the kitchen and the yard.*

Ruth   I have decided, actually. To leave – David.

Marian   Take your coat off.

Ruth   It was . . . rather sudden. I'll need to get, you know . . . get my things, tomorrow. It was just, tonight, I couldn't think, where else . . . he might try . . . (*Yawns.*) . . . he wouldn't know . . . down here's the last place he'd think.

Marian   Just sit down. (*Guiding her into the rocking-chair.*) Ruth – there's blood seeping through this, I'm going to take it off . . .

Ruth   No, no, leave it, it's nothing, I just gave my head a crack . . .

Marian   I'm taking it off, Ruth.

Ruth   (*clinging to the bandanna*) . . . getting out of the car it was, just a bump, honest . . .

Marian   (*sharply*)   Let go! (*She begins to undo the bandanna.*)

Ruth   Oh, no, it's not, it's not . . . oh, no, no, oh no, oh no, no no no no no . . . (*It has developed into an uncontrollable cry, her whole body rocking back and forward.*) . . . oh no . . . no . . . NO!

Marian   (*as she struggles with the bandanna*)   All right, Ruth. It's okay. You're all right now.

*She gets the bandanna off to reveal a livid, glistening purplish-red weal slantwise across **Ruth**'s forehead, and her hair wet with blood.*

Ruth   No . . . No . . . NO!

Marian   (*holding her hands*)   It's all over. You're safe now. You're safe here. Easy, now. Hold on, Ruth. I'm just going to get something for that wound.

She runs out to the bathroom. **Ruth** *begins to quieten.* **Marian** *returns, clutching* **Lily Matthews'** *old-fashioned wooden first-aid box. She takes out lint and antiseptic and proceeds to clean* **Ruth**'s *wounds during the continuing dialogue.*

Marian   Okay. This should sort you out. It looks to me like army surplus from the Dardanelles campaign. Definitely guaranteed to separate the women from the girls. (*As she swabs the wound.*) Does that hurt?

Ruth (*nodding*)   Unh.

Marian   Terrific. What in God's name did he hit you with? The lawnmower or what?

Ruth   The, the . . . truncheon . . .

Marian (*stopping work*)   His police truncheon? He took that to you?

Ruth *starts to sob again a little.*

Marian   All right, all right, as you were. We'll have to get this X-rayed, there could easily be concussion . . .

Ruth   There's no . . . no . . .

Marian   Is your sight blurred?

Ruth   No. Never fainted.

Marian   Well. We'll see about that in the morning. I'll put you in Lily's bed tonight, I can kip down here. It's a lot warmer anyhow.

Ruth   I'm – sorry.

Marian   Lily's our hostess here, in case you're wondering. Lily Matthews. It's her house. All her gear. I haven't touched anything, I don't want anything tidied up or touched, Ruth, that's the one stipulation I have to make, about you staying here.

Ruth   Is she not . . . dead?

Marian   She was the same age as the century. Born

1900. Married 1918. Dispossessed – for the first time anyway – 1921.

Ruth   How do you know?

Marian   I've started going through her belongings. Her whole life's here, all intact. Her husband died in 1959. She changed not a single detail from then till the day she died herself, two months ago. (*Finishing her ministrations.*) There. That should keep you healthy for a bit longer. How does it feel?

Ruth   Okay.

Marian   Yeah, like a bandaged migraine. Time for that drink now. (*Producing brandy.*) For me, I mean. Not that you can't join me if you absolutely insist on it.

She takes a swig, hands it to **Ruth** *who pours a capful and drinks it from the cap. They stare into the fire for a bit.*

Ruth   Remember your flat. Magdala Street. Calling round. Always the big fire. Out would come the bottle.

Marian   Rough cider in those days, girl. (*Picking up the brandy bottle.*) That's the one thing that's tangibly improved. In the intervening decade.

She swigs. They stare into the fire.

Ruth   We haven't done – all that well, have we.

Marian   Speak for yourself.

Ruth   Sorry.

Marian   Joke.

Ruth *consciously rallies herself for the next bit.*

Ruth   I know what you think of David . . .

Marian   Don't talk to me about it.

Ruth   Please, Marian.

Marian   You said you'd left him, sound move. Stick to it. He's behind you now, receding over the horizon.

Bye-bye David. There he goes. Good riddance.

Ruth The way you did with Lenny, I suppose.

Marian Lenny played that godawful noise, on that trombone of his, half the night, it was enough to give you a splitting headache, certainly – however, he never actually smashed me across the skull with it.

Ruth You can't even begin to imagine the pressure the police are under . . .

Marian I don't want to get into it, Ruth.

Ruth I'm not making excuses for him.

Marian He's a policeman, who strikes his wife, about the head, with his own truncheon, there are no excuses.

Ruth I know that.

Marian No imaginable excuses, I'm talking fractured skulls, brain damage, haemorrhages – he could have killed you!

Ruth He's not a bad person, Marian, honest to God, his nerves are frayed away to nothing . . .

Marian Forget it.

Ruth They never know the minute, he's had three good mates killed in his own station, and a fourth one blinded, it's the waiting around all day that gets to him, all the threats and the hatred and no outlet, he comes home coiled up like a spring, he's frightened of his life, it's all pent up inside him . . . Christ, I'm no better, sitting at home, waiting to hear the worst . . . I caught my sleeve on one of his swimming trophies – Waterford crystal it was – it smashed to bits in the hearth . . . I just stared down stupid at the pieces like a child who knows it's in for a thumping . . . it was a sort of blinding crunch and a flash of light, I was lying behind the sofa then and I could feel my hair getting wet . . . twice more he hit me . . . but I had my arms up by then . . .

the phone started to ring, I think that saved me, not
that he answered it, it sort of half brought him round,
he just stared down at me and said, 'that's you sorted
out', and then he threw the truncheon into a corner and
went into the hall for his coat and I heard the front
door slamming. He hadn't even had his dinner. So I got
up and cleaned myself off – I knew then I had to go,
get away – I didn't want to be there when he got back,
not this time – I really knew this time I couldn't live
with him any more – how can you love somebody once
you're actually in fear of your life of him – I don't
blame him, Marian, but I can't stay with him, I can't
stand being so scared . . . I'm sorry.

Marian *is staring into the fire.* **Ruth** *pours herself another
capful of brandy.*

Ruth   God. Look at us. Magdala Street.

Marian   Scarcely.

Ruth   All over again. Isn't it?

Marian   Not exactly.

Ruth   All those nights, landing in on you . . .
boyfriends usually, it was . . .

Marian   One boyfriend, it was.

Ruth   If it wasn't the shorthand and typing course. Oh
well.

Marian   He was clouting you even then, Ruth.

Ruth   It was forever me crying my eyes out anyhow.

Marian   Even as the boyfriend he was at it.

Ruth   Always some thing or another.

Marian   He started it then. He started it right at the
beginning. Before the troubles were ever heard of, well
before he joined the police, this has nothing to do with
the police. He was handing you out a regular hiding,

even then, that was what brought you crying to me, night in night out, only you never owned up to it, you covered up for the bastard till you had your first miscarriage for which he was to blame . . .

Ruth   It's not true!

Marian   The lies you've told for the sake of that sadistic pig . . .

Ruth   Who are you . . . ?

Marian   Ten years of it.

Ruth   What have you got to show?

Marian   I said I didn't want to get into it.

Ruth   He's no pig, he's a human being!

Marian   All right. Enough.

Ruth   We had fights, everybody has fights, maybe you didn't, married to that pathetic piss-artist . . .

Marian   You want to stay here?

Ruth   Lenny Harrigan was a gutless dropout fit-for-nothing from the day and hour you met him, my David's out there on those streets day and night risking his life to protect other people . . .

Marian   He's done a really impressive job for you.

Ruth   If you're so very superior, Marian, what exactly are you doing here, sitting here, in a condemned slum, at one in the morning, completely alone, sitting here staring into that fire, drinking on your own, if you know so much more, just show us what it is, the secret of your massive fucking success, because the rest of us would love to know, what it is we're doing, patronising and protecting your antiques business and your husband who abandoned his law degree and has been sponging off the state ever since and his daddy the Catholic barrister who makes a fat living out of finding loopholes in the law for

Republican mass murderers to slip through, and your intellectual IRA friends who're busy liberating us from our legs and our brains and our children, just tell us . . . who in hell you are . . . to sit in judgement, all the time . . .

Marian   You want to stay here?

Ruth   I'm sorry.

Marian   You still want to stay?

Ruth   I'm like . . . something wild . . .

Marian   Because ground rules are needed here. There are things to bear in mind here. Such as. This is the third time you've left David and come running to me.

Ruth   Marian, don't be angry. I'm really sorry, honest to God . . .

Marian   The previous two times you went back to him. I'm beginning to feel like the other woman. With all the aggravation and no sex.

Ruth   I won't be going back again.

Marian   Where will you live?

Ruth   I – plan to find a flat.

Marian   Tomorrow? (**Ruth** *hesitates.*) You can't live here.

Ruth   No, of course, it was just for tonight, I couldn't think where else . . . I mean, if it's a problem . . .

Marian   It's a problem. (*She sustains her level stare at* **Ruth**, *who looks away.*) I'm hardly going to throw you out on the street, am I. Tomorrow you find a flat.

Ruth   I said. Look, I could easily sleep in the front parlour, that way I'd be no trouble at all . . .

Marian   You're not sleeping in Lily's parlour, she has the dust sheets on still. You'll be in her bedroom.

Ruth   Thank you.

Marian   Concerning the other matters, Ruth – the heavy burden of my antiques business which you feel that you've been carrying . . .

Ruth   Please, Marian . . .

Marian   The shop has in fact been taken over by Tom Feeney, the gallery owner, who has impeccably Protestant credentials as of course you well know. Lenny, just for the record, hasn't actually had to draw the dole since receiving an annuity from the same maiden aunt who left him this house in her will, the two friends I had who joined the Republican movement are no longer friends, on account of one being dead and the other being a pious fool who's now in Long Kesh and deserves to stay there, Lenny isn't entirely my husband since we're halfway through a divorce, and I can hardly be held responsible for his da who, amongst other things, was always avid to achieve purchase on my inner thigh over the Christmas period . . .

Ruth   I remember.

Marian   Generally speaking, Ruth, in regard to these ground rules, whereas you may be a girlhood friend, you're nobody's probation officer, and if I choose to drink brandy in front of a fire in a house eloquent with the history of this city at a time of the night when I feel most sensate, that's a choice I'm making out of my own free will under my own control for my own pleasure which is a private decision not subject to invasion by anyone whatsoever . . .

The sound of someone opening and coming through the front door is heard from offstage.

Ruth   Oh my God!

Marian (*leaping up*)   Quiet!

She grabs a poker from the fireplace and positions herself by the

*kitchen door, on the non-opening side. The door is flung open –
concealing* **Marian** *from view altogether – and* **Lenny** *enters,
precipitously, since he is carrying two bulging holdalls and has his
trombone case under one arm.*

Lenny   Ruth? – how did you get here? What
happened to your head?

Marian *reveals herself by pushing the door shut.* **Lenny**
registers the poker.

Lenny   Have you two been fighting each other?

Marian   What's this all about?

Lenny   Who did you imagine I was?

Marian   What are these bags?

Lenny   I've been totally burgled. The entire place,
stripped clean. I was out playing at a gig. My house is
like a bomb site. Well – nearly.

Marian   You're not planning on staying here?

Lenny   It's really very kind of you to sympathise,
Marian – but I expect I'll get over it in time.

Ruth   Did you notify the police?

Lenny   Usual formalities. They are a bit otherwise
engaged – hardly news to you.

Marian   Ruth's already staying tonight.

Lenny   Fine. Lovely. A few more arrivals and we can
throw a party.

Marian   There's nowhere for you to sleep.

Lenny   Marian – I could begin to feel a trifle testy at
your demeanour.

Ruth   I'll make us some tea. (*She hurries out of the
hostilities into the scullery, and proceeds to put the kettle on.*)

Lenny   I get home after midnight to find that

everything of value I possess has been stolen, right down to the brass bed, which is particularly inconvenient since I normally use it for sleeping on . . .

Marian   There's plenty of beds in your parents' house.

Lenny   What the hell do you think you're doing here anyway?

Marian   Looking for a quiet life, quaint as that may sound to you.

Lenny   Who said you could move in, the house doesn't belong to you, not yet.

Marian   We've exchanged contracts.

Lenny   We haven't completed!

Marian   Don't start on the legalese, we've both agreed I'm buying the house, so I'm living here now and I don't want you poking your head round the door any time the fancy takes you.

Lenny   What do you imagine this is, some clever ploy to worm my way back in beneath your panty-hose, forget it – not interested.

Marian   Not on offer if you were.

Lenny   Good, that's a relief. So. You and your friend want to camp out overnight in my house, is that it?

Marian   Fuck off.

Lenny   Well, you're most welcome to, yes, certainly. First up makes breakfast. (*Calling through the door.*) Find everything you need there, Ruth?

Ruth   Thanks, Lenny, yes.

Lenny   Great stuff. (*Sotto voce to* **Marian**.) What's Desdemona doing here exactly?

Marian   Another refugee.

Lenny   Did he give her that head?

Marian   She's left him.

Lenny   Not again. He'll be the next one through the door, then. Just like old times, really.

Marian   Not in any respect whatsoever.

Lenny   Where's she sleeping?

Marian   Lily's bed.

Lenny   You?

Marian   In front of this fire.

Lenny   The top bedroom for me then.

Marian   The bedding's damp.

Lenny (*picking up one of the holdalls*)   Sleeping bag.

Marian   Thoughtful of the burglars to leave you that.

Lenny   It's yours, actually. It was under the stairs.

Marian   Great. I can use it for in here ... (*Takes the holdall, unzips it, removes the sleeping bag.*)

Lenny   Just bear in mind, Marian – I can have you evicted from this house. If I had a mind to do it, I could still call off the sale.

Marian   I've moved in. I'm here to stay. Try it.

Lenny   You know – I was left in bits after you walked out on me. Except for enormous relief about one thing. Which I've never stopped thanking God for. I didn't have to attempt to understand you any more.

Marian   Well, I'm run ragged, Lenny. From understanding you through and through.

Ruth (*calling through to them*)   Tea's nearly ready!

Lenny   Scrub it, Ruth. I think you'll find the milk's all curdled.

He picks up his luggage and exits upstairs.

Ruth   Will I use these mugs?

Marian   No. Leave them.

Ruth   Where are the cups?

Marian   I don't want any tea. You can use the kettle for a hot-water bottle. You're going to need one, in that bedroom.

Ruth   Right-o.

She looks around the scullery for it, then returns to the kitchen door in a helpless kind of way.

Marian   It's on the back of the door.

Ruth *mutely fetches it.* **Marian** *has sat down again in the rocking-chair and is staring into the fire. From upstairs, the sound of* **Lenny** *playing his trombone starts up: loud and up-tempo. She looks slowly up at the ceiling at the sound. The lights fade to blackout.*

Scene Three

*The night of Sunday, 19 May. The kitchen and scullery are dark and deserted. The sound of half a dozen drunken youths running up the back entry, shouting and whistling, is heard from off. A beer bottle sails over the yard wall and smashes harmlessly on the floor of the yard. Then silence returns. Until the front door can be heard opening and two slightly drunk men (***Lenny** *and* **Peter***) coming into the hall.*

Lenny (*offstage*)   Easy on.

Peter (*offstage*)   Bloody blind man's buff . . .

Lenny   Sshh . . . (*Calling out.*) Fear not, ladies, it's reinforcements. You can put the poker away!

Sound of **Peter** *laughing and then stumbling.*

Lenny   Watch the bottles, for God's sake . . .

Peter   Well, get some lights on . . .

The kitchen door is thrust open, to reveal **Lenny** *carrying a cardboard box full of beer cans and bottles of spirits. He gropes round for the light switch with his free hand, makes contact, and the electric light comes on.*

Lenny   What do you know, we're in luck, head. Double luck. The electricity is on and the housemother is absent. We've got power without responsibility.

Peter *has followed him into the room, carrying a tray, a bag and a bulky paper sack, like a small bag of cement. His style is 1974 casual chic.*

Peter   My drinking arm's gone dead with the weight of this stuff.

He dumps the heavy sack down along with his travel bag.

Lenny   What did you have to hump that muck across the water for anyhow?

Peter   It's muesli. Grain and nuts, honey, dried fruit . . .

Lenny   It has been heard of here, you know, you don't actually have to define it.

Peter   Didn't want to use up your food supplies.

Lenny   You've brought about three stone of it.

Peter   It's very nutritious, I figured I could live on it, if the strike goes on indefinitely, do you think it might?

Lenny   You need milk.

Peter   This is true.

Lenny   You can't eat it without milk. Is what I'm saying.

Peter   Ah, holy God, they haven't stopped the milk,

have they?

Lenny   Peter, use the loaf – protest strike by Loyalist workers, right? Electricity cuts. No petrol supplies. No animal foodstuffs. Barricades all over the city turning back the traffic. Three quarters of all cows are Protestant. What chance has the milk got?

Peter (*who has been holding out his right arm, wincing*)   Pins and needles.

Lenny *opens a can of beer from the box.*

Lenny   Here. Try it left-handed. As they say in the Marriage Guidance counsel.

Peter   Do they?

Lenny   More or less.

Peter   Well, you should know. Cheers.

Lenny   And welcome home to you, old fruit.

They drink.

Peter   Do I sound very English?

Lenny   Yeah, but only when you talk.

Peter   Don't you just love it – the sly dig, the dry remark, how painfully I've missed it. The authentic Lilliputian wit. (*Moving round, surveying the rooms.*) And this is the inheritance?

Lenny   It's the best I can do for you tonight.

Peter   An ethnic little gem, though. What? Set this load down in a choicer part of Birmingham, a treasure trove is what you'd have, my son, a highly des. res. in need of minor gentrification.

Lenny   You're welcome to ship the whole lot back with you, I can't believe you managed to get over here. Or why.

Peter I did have to hang about most of the night, it's true – waiting for the blasted ferry to make up its mind to sail from Heysham.

Lenny There can only have been you on it.

Peter Well, aside from a coach party of foreign travel agents, and a young soldier's wife.

Lenny No doubt you took care of her.

Peter Once she got her horrible kids to sleep. It was the travel agents who were really in need of looking after, though. Wholesale shitlessness.

Lenny How did you get the booze?

Peter Bribed the barman.

Lenny Jesus. See you, head? People like you lead a charmed life. If I hadn't just chanced to sneak across town this evening . . . you do realise it's mob law here at the minute?

Peter I've been watching it all week. The BBC have adapted it for television, you know.

Lenny I haven't been living in my own place for nearly a month, since the burglary, I hadn't even set foot in it in the last four days, since the strike got heavy – it was a pure fluke, showing up there tonight, just in time to bump into you. Anybody but you could have been in a tightish corner.

Peter I placed my faith in the Ulster Sunday. I believed in my heart, brother – even if the Protestant blackshirts had finally staged a putsch, they would still remember the seventh day and keep it holy. Not to mention rainy, bleak, doom-laden, and utterly devoid of human life. Sure enough. I was able to roam at will around the mean streets – apart from the occasional catcall, and comment of a personal nature.

Lenny You didn't want to miss all the stir, I suppose.

Peter   It sounds to me like the big picture. The '74 Uprising. The Great Loyalist Insurrection. Historic Days in Lilliput.

Lenny   Sure, every bloody day in the week's historic, in this place.

Peter   Anyway, I was due a trip home. It's been three years.

Lenny   You're not going to go on calling it Lilliput the whole time?

Peter   What, this teeny weeny wee province of ours and its little people, all the angry munchkins, with their midget brains, this festering pimple on the vast white flabby bum of western Europe, what would *you* call it?

Lenny   I call it home.

Peter   You do realise – the rest of the world has crossed the street, long since, passed on by – on account of having fully-grown twentieth-century problems to be getting on with – the continued existence of the planet, say, or the survival of the species?

Lenny   So is that what they fight about in Birmingham?

Peter   What am I hearing? For God's sake don't tell me you've turned into a proud wee Ulsterman?

Lenny   Coals to Newcastle, okay? Coals of fire, in this case, you get them heaped on your head here every time you turn round. The last thing I need is you landing in and dumping another load on me.

Peter   Only the truth. Crass insensitivity. Craven apologies. Not another slur against the dear wee darling homeland shall pass these lips.

Lenny   It's the arsehole of hell, who's arguing. No future in it. Whatsoever. Once this Prod agitation is over, I'm off out, I've definitely had enough, I know what you're going to say.

Peter   All right – but apart from that . . .

Lenny   What? Apart from what?

Peter   Apart from the fact that you've said it all a dozen times before . . .

Lenny   Dammit, Peter, I knew that's what you were going to say!

Peter   I wasn't going to say it, you asked me to say it.

Lenny   I'm serious, I mean it.

Peter   All right.

Lenny   Things have changed. Is what I'm saying.

Peter   All right. Always assuming it ever will be over, of course.

Lenny   What? The strike? 'Course it will.

Peter   Strike? This is no strike. (*Paisleyite voice.*) This is a constitutional stoppage!

Lenny   God save us, Doctor, that sounds agonising, is there nothing you could prescribe that would shift it?

Peter   I mean, what if they do take over, for keeps? They'll throw all you Fenian rebels into the Gulag – make you earn your supplementary benefit sewing mailbags.

Lenny   What makes you think you'd be let off?

Peter   Me, I'm one of the elect – my daddy's even a minister of the true faith.

Lenny   You're joking, he's a Methodist. Out on the barricades there, that counts as dangerous left-wing subversion. Your da's ecumenical!

Peter   All right, keep your voice down.

Lenny   Anyhow, with that hair and those jeans, and the way you talk – not to mention the muesli –

Peter   All right, all right. I've got the gag.

Lenny   Never you fret, head, it'll be over within the week.

Peter   Somebody on the boat was saying they'd declared a state of emergency . . .

Lenny   Meaning the army's finally going to be ordered to break it. The English have just been hanging on as usual, waiting for reason and moderation and fair play to break out suddenly – you know – just like it always does in the Houses of Parliament.

Peter (*parliamentary braying*)   Heah heah, heah heah heah . . .

Lenny (*joining in*)   Heah heah heah . . . (*Laughs.*) . . . yeah, right. So anyhow. You still like it over there?

Peter   It's a lot bigger.

Lenny   Well. This is it. (*A gap has opened in the banter.*)

Peter   And how about you? You're actually going to attempt the great escape this time?

Lenny   Nothing to keep me here now. Apart from three hundred-odd street barricades, and thousands of hooded men with clubs.

The front door being opened is heard from off.

Peter   Is that Marian?

Lenny   Look, just remember what I told you, right?

Peter   I'm cool.

Lenny   Leave her to me.

Peter   All yours.

They are all tensed up in anticipation of the onslaught. The door from the hall opens and **Ruth** *enters, carrying a heavy bale of peat briquettes in one hand and a Bible in the other. She is dressed in her Sunday best.*

Ruth   Sorry . . .

Lenny   Ah, Ruth. It's you.

Ruth   Look what Marian's mother gave us. For the fire.

Lenny   Did Marian come back with you?

Ruth   She's just parking her car. Up behind our church. There's a car park there.

Lenny   Good thinking.

Ruth   It's a bit safer.

Peter   I'm glad to hear those old buildings are being put to some practical use.

Ruth   It's the Church of God, it was only built last year.

Lenny   By the way, Ruth, this here is a friend of mine from student days, Peter Irwin. (*To the latter.*) This is Ruth MacAlester.

Ruth (*as she sets the bale of peat down in the hearth*)   How'd you do.

Peter   Fancy a beer?

Ruth   I have to change, excuse me. (*She exits, up the stairs.*)

Peter   Protestant nookie, in the house, why wasn't I informed.

Lenny   She was supposed to be moving to her ma's this morning.

Peter   Not a bad arse on her.

Lenny   Forget it, she's one of Marian's lame ducks.

Peter   Not the cop's wife again?

Lenny   She left him three weeks ago, serious GBH. She's been holed up here ever since.

Peter   My God, so you've been besieged, all this time, with not just one but two frigid cows – lucky I turned up, head. You're in serious need of reinforcements.

Lenny   Listen. Go easy with Marian.

Peter   What? I haven't even clapped eyes on her yet.

Lenny   I know how to handle her, it's just, when she sees you here – she's definitely going to cut up rough.

Peter   Sure. Yeah. Marian and me were never exactly a mutual admiration society.

Lenny   It's not that, it's the state she's in . . . totally obsessive, don't ask me what the story is . . . some weird syndrome, you know how it is with women. I'm just thankful she's finally agreed to a divorce.

Peter   Would it still be losing the kid, maybe?

Lenny   That? – oh, she took that in her stride . . . didn't she . . . no problem. Anyhow. It's five years now.

Peter   Can't be.

Lenny   Near as dammit. August '69.

Peter   A vintage month.

Lenny   The marriage started to go dead too, from then on.

Peter   Bound to. The pair of you had never intended to hitch up in the first place. Not until the pregnancy.

Lenny   Yeah, but let me tell you a funny story. When the sprog was born – Christopher, to give him his due and proper name – the bunched-up fingers and feet, like tight fat buds, flailing away at us . . . when he was there between us on the bed, all crinkled-up and livid . . .

something out of order happened. Between Marian and me. We sort of fell in love. With each other. At least I know I did, she would sneer at all that now, don't ever let me catch you breathing a word of this . . .

Peter   Swear.

Lenny   . . . I'd stake my life on it, if you really want to know, so there we were. Married lovers, the way it's always supposed to be in the booklets. It wasn't exactly a pleasure trip, there was very little sleep, money was tight, we didn't get out a lot. It's the one time so far I've ever felt one hundred per cent alive. For five months. That was how long it lasted . . . that was how long the sprog lasted. At that point he checked out, he'd seen enough. Maybe it was the prospect of having me as a da, you could hardly blame him . . . she came down in the morning . . . the cot was still, no more fury . . . just a tiny silent shrivelled-up rickle of bones and skin. She came and woke me. She took it in her stride. I picked him up . . . you didn't know this. Any of it. He was my son. She was my wife.

Peter *is left at a loss for a few moments. Then he fetches a can of beer from the box, opens it and offers it to* **Lenny**. **Lenny** *takes it and drinks deep. The sound of somebody coming in from the street is heard from off. After a moment,* **Marian** *enters from the hall, in church-going clothes also, carrying a bag of dry foods.*

Marian   My God.

Peter   Hello there, Marian.

Marian   The lulu's back in town. How did you get here?

Peter   Oh, you know – the spirit moved me.

Marian   So how long has the spirit dumped you here for?

Peter   That's really up to the Ulster Workers' Council.

Marian   Hang on a minute. You went off and qualified as a property surveyor. Is that right?

Peter   It's what pays the rent.

Marian   I imagine it does. You need a place to stay?

Lenny   In actual point of fact . . .

Marian   Here's an offer. You can have the boxroom upstairs for a week. In return for doing me a professional full-scale written structural survey of the house.

Peter   What for?

Marian   What do you say?

Peter   If you like.

Marian   I've got some people coming from the National Trust on Thursday, that's when you have to do it by. Deal?

Peter   Fine.

Marian   Very good, Peter, glad you managed back.

She moves on into the kitchen to unload her bag.

Lenny   Hold it just a minute. What has the National Trust got to do with anything?

Marian   Very little, in your case.

Peter (*to* **Marian**)   Is the survey meant to be shown to them or something?

Marian   Given to them.

Peter   Why on earth?

Marian   Because I'm making them an offer too. To take over this house as a National Trust property.

Lenny   Take over – here? This?

It's too much for him, he lets out a bellow of incredulous laughter.

Peter *grimaces at him to be quiet and moves to the kitchen door.*

Peter (*to* **Marian**)   Is it really – their style, though? Marian? Would you say? The National Trust?

Marian   Not yet, it isn't.

Peter   I mean, it certainly does have plenty of atmosphere . . .

Lenny   God knows, fish could nearly swim in it.

Peter   It's just, you know – all those Castle Coole and Castleward types of places . . .

Lenny   It's all those fully upholstered la-di-da lady baritones, Jesus wept, can you imagine them in here, selling postcards of the outside bog and knitted tea cosies?

Marian   I'm glad I'm keeping you entertained.

Peter   Where on earth did you get the idea, Marian?

Marian   Lily Matthews lived here. 1900 to 1974. This house was her whole life. She never threw anything away. I've started cataloguing it all. Every last thimble and shirt stud, every grocery bill and cigarette card and rationing coupon, every document of her and Alfie's life together. (*She scoops up some documents from a shoe box on the sideboard.*) Look at this – the dismissal from his gasfitting job in 1931. They were able to manage through the Depression by finding a lodger to take in – that's his rent book there. Alan Ferris. He was an English airman. His photograph's here. The three of them together. (*She carefully scrutinises the photograph.*)

Peter   Right. Yeah. Though, there must be thousands of houses like this . . . thousands of people, like that. It's very touching, absolutely – but it's nothing special, though. Is it?

Marian   You think not? So why should Lily Matthews' home and hearth be less special than Lord Castlereagh's or the Earl of Enniskillen's? A whole way of life, a whole culture, the only difference being, that this home speaks for a far greater community of experience in this country than some transplanted feeble-minded aristocrat's ever could, have you looked at it, properly?

Peter   Haven't had a chance yet.

Marian   Never mind what you learnt as a student architect, this is what design and building and history mean, to the people of this city, go ahead. Look around it. Just don't touch anything, I've changed nothing. Lenny, show him where the boxroom is.

Lenny   Why can't he sleep in the front parlour?

Marian   It's a front parlour, that's why.

Lenny   Exactly. Instead of being a boxroom.

Peter   Why don't I just take my gear upstairs, while I'm at it. (*Picking up his travel bag and making an exit out the hall door and up the stairs.*)

Lenny (*to* **Marian**)   The National Trust ... you're not actually serious?

Marian   No more refugees. There are three too many as it is.

Lenny (*gesturing towards the bag*)   Help yourself to the muesli.

He exits in pursuit of **Peter**. **Marian** *closes the door behind them. She crosses to the rocking-chair, sits down in it, and stares into the empty grate. From the far distance, the sound of two lambeg drums head-to-head starts up.* **Lily Matthews** *appears from the pantry. She comes right into the kitchen, to behind the rocking-chair. She looks to be in late middle age now, but wearing a pretty print dress from the early thirties with a pinafore over it, and her hair drawn up in a bun.*

Lily   You needn't bother getting settled. You'll have no peace in this house, nor good fortune neither.

Marian What kind of fortune did you have, Lily?

Lily Four of yous now, in on me, tramping your filth all over my good floors.

Marian We'll have it back to ourselves, you and me, soon enough. Back to rights.

Lily You've been to your mass again, I can smell it off you.

Marian Something I've been meaning to ask you . . .

Lily Why did you come here? What possessed you to move in on me?

Marian Fifteen years, all on your own. The neighbours leaving one by one, blind houses blocked up behind them, the street gradually silenced. Shut up in here. The loneliness of it.

Lily I had my own people round me, never wanted for anything.

Marian I've been lonely myself, you see.

Lily Never wanted company . . .

Marian Five years now.

Lily Quite content on my own, thank you.

Marian That's why.

Lily Up until you turned up. Four of yous now, in on me.

Marian Company like that only makes you lonelier, you think I don't understand that, you think I want them here either?

Lily Don't you imagine you can find favour with me, dear, when you couldn't even make a decent life with your own husband, your own sort.

Marian That's the dress you were wearing in that photograph.

Lily   Stay you out of my private belongings!

Marian   In the name of Jesus I'm trying to preserve them!

Lily   Don't you dare blaspheme in my kitchen!

Marian   Sorry, I'm sorry . . .

Lily   Nobody asked your help and it's not wanted.

Marian   It's not help that I'm offering . . . it's help that I'm looking for. Is that not obvious?

Lily *begins to sing.*

Lily   Oh, God our help in ages past . . .

Marian   Don't fight me, Lily . . .

Lily (*continuing to sing over* **Marian**'s *lines*)
  Our hope for years to come . . .

Marian   I need you, we have got to make this work, you and me . . .

Lily (*singing on regardless*)
  Our shelter from the stormy blast,
  And our eternal home!

Marian   You think you're haunting me, don't you. But you see it's me that's actually haunting you. I'm not going to go away. There's no curse or hymn that can exorcise me. So you might as well just give me your blessing and make your peace with me, Lily.

Lily   You'll have no peace in this house.

Marian   Why had you no wee 'uns? You weren't able, was that it?

Lily   Never had a day's sickness in my life, there was nothing the matter with me or mine.

Marian   So it was Alfie, then?

Lily   That's no business of yours or of your like, my
Alfie was a good man, he would have made a loving
father, if the Good Lord didn't see fit to send us a little
one, so be it, he giveth and he taketh away, blessed be
the name of the Lord. Anyway, I haven't noticed you
bringing up any youngsters.

Marian   No. The Lord didn't do too well by me
either. In that respect.

Lily   What right does a hussy like you have, to
question God's will? Why would he bless the fruit of
your womb more than mine, look at this place, you
have it like a pigsty ... are there not enough runty
litters running the streets, whelped by your kind, reared
with a half-brick in their fists, and the backsides hanging
out of their trousers?

Marian *has reached into the raffia basket tucked in by the side
of the rocking-chair.*

Marian   It was just that I found this.

*She takes out and holds up a 1930s child's christening gown,
trimmed with lace and ribbons.*

Lily *(terrified)*   The devil ...

Marian   Folded up.

Lily   The devil is in this house ...

Marian   Wrapped in tissue.

Lily   The Antichrist is in our midst!

Marian   Hidden amongst your underwear.

Lily *backs away into the scullery.*

Lily   Oh, Lord Jesus, send the devil out of this room,
let your servant now depart in peace ... *(She is melting
into the shadows once again.)*

Ruth *comes in from the hall.*

Ruth   Is he away?

Marian   What? Who?

Ruth   The friend of Lenny's. Peter.

Marian   He's staying here.

Ruth (*seeing the christening robe*)   Och, look, isn't that the loveliest thing ... was it hers? I thought there were no children?

Marian   Maybe she lived in hope. Like you and me.

Ruth   Not me, Marian. Not now.

Marian   You're not even thirty. There's a whole life to come.

Ruth   They don't think ... after I lost the third one ... they told me that ... it mightn't ...

Marian   It's a childless house. Barren. Why else would I feel so much at home.

Ruth   What do you know about it, yours was alive, at least you had it at your breast, for a while at least, you knew what it was, oh Jesus if only I'd been able to keep just one of them, to hold it back to make it grow, we'd be all right, all different, if I can't have a child I won't live!

Marian   Christopher would have been five in August. Starting school. If he hadn't gone. Left me. Given up the ghost in me. My own soul, left for dead. He was our future, you see. Future, at a time like this ... what could it possibly mean – a future? In a place like this?

She looks down at **Lily***'s unused christening robe.* **Ruth** *goes to her, kneels by her, embraces her. The light fades to blackout, on the grief of the three women.*

Act Two

Scene One

The night of Saturday, 25 May. The house is in darkness. Over the theatre PA we hear the opening of a broadcast to the nation being given by the Prime Minister, Harold Wilson.

Broadcast tape   As this holiday weekend begins, Northern Ireland faces the gravest crisis in her history. It is a crisis equally for all of us who live on this side of the water. What we are seeing in Northern Ireland is not just an industrial strike. It has nothing to do with wages. It has nothing to do with jobs – except to imperil jobs. It is a deliberate and calculated attempt to use every undemocratic and unparliamentary means for the purpose of bringing down the whole constitution of Northern Ireland so as to set up there a sectarian and undemocratic state . . .

Ruth *has come into the kitchen from the hall, with a lighted candle in one hand and a transistor radio in the other. The sound of the broadcast from her radio overlaps with and soon takes over from the theatre PA.*

Radio   . . . We recognise that behind this situation lie many genuine and deeply held fears. I have to say that these fears are unfounded. That they are being deliberately fostered by people in search of power.

Peter *has followed* **Ruth** *into the kitchen, carrying a lighted oil lamp. She has set her candle down on the mantelpiece and the radio on the table, and has sat down to listen. He places the oil lamp on the sideboard, and also sits down to listen.*

Radio   The people on this side of the water – British parents – have seen their sons vilified and spat upon and murdered. British taxpayers have seen the taxes they have poured out, almost without regard to cost – over

three hundred million pounds this year with the cost of
the Army operation on top of that – going into
Northern Ireland. They see property destroyed by evil
violence and are asked to pick up the bill for rebuilding
it. Yet people who benefit from all this now viciously
defy Westminster, purporting to act as though they were
an elected government; people who spend their lives
sponging on Westminster and British democracy and
then systematically assault democratic methods. Who do
these people think they are?

Ruth *springs up in a fury and switches the radio off.*

Peter   Hey.

Ruth   How dare he?

Peter   He hasn't finished.

Ruth   How dare he say that to us? – *us* – spongers!

Peter   What's the odds?

Ruth   We worked hard for everything we have and
hold, we're British taxpayers just the same as they are!

Peter   He's talking about the seizing of power!

Ruth   This city was full of life, full of industry, built by
our people, they made it into a capital city, to be proud
of . . .

Peter   All right.

Ruth   Everything we have and hold, for five long years
now we've watched it rent asunder, pulverised into
rubble by the real spongers, cruel and murderous
bastards . . .

Peter   All right!

Ruth   How long are we supposed to grin and bear it?

Peter   I haven't noticed much grinning.

Ruth We've had enough, far more than enough.

Peter So this is your idea of a solution?

Ruth Something had to be done!

Peter No food, no light, no heat, the bullet-heads in charge?

Ruth That smug wee English shite with his weaselly voice, what right has he to lecture us, he'll soon know his driver, the same boyo . . .

Peter He isn't here, Ruthie child, he's five hundred-odd miles in that direction, over the sea, fully fed and comfortable, this is being done to us, the people here, self-inflicted, is this what you want? – the apemen in charge, shops without food to sell, garages without petrol, people penned into their own homes, cold hungry and terrified, there's a mile-long queue of doctors and nurses and social workers, and lawyers, up at Hawthornden Road, queuing up to beg for a special pass to get them through the barricades to their patients and clients, and from who? – from the wee hard men who can barely sign their name to their special bloody passes, from shipyard Bible-thumpers, unemployed binmen, petty crooks and extortionists, pigbrain mobsters and thugs, they've seized control over all of us, they're now ordering the sewage workers out, the raw sewage is about to come flooding down those streets out there, and it won't be the English who die of typhoid, Ruth, this is not what we call a protest movement, this is what is historically known as root-and-branch fascism . . .

Ruth Just shut up and listen for a minute!

Peter We're at the mercy of actual real-life fascist jackboot rule!

Ruth Use your ears, just listen. Out there. Right? Nothing. No gunplay. No bombs. How long is it – how long, since you could go to sleep at night, without that?

Of course you wouldn't know, would you.

Peter   What does that prove?

Ruth   The IRA have been stopped in their tracks at last.

Peter   For Christ's sake, they're on hold, that's all, you're doing it all for them, alienate the Brits, that broadcast was like music to their ears, are you deaf, blind and entirely thick?

Ruth   Don't you condescend to me . . .

Peter   Can you not see, this whole tribe, so-called Protestants, we both of us grew up in it, all that endless mindless marching, they've been marching away with the lambegs blattering and the banners flying straight up a dead-end one-way blind alley, self-destroying, the head's eating the tail now, it's a lingering tribal suicide going on out there, there was no need for any of it, they held all the cards, they only needed to be marginally generous, how did I get into this, I apologise for what I called you, I got carried away, fear no doubt, funny isn't it . . . it's not as if I'm unfamiliar with tense situations. Six years ago, I was standing in a human chain encircling a building. It was in America . . . a university. Black students had seized the building and smuggled in guns, the police were lined up in their hundreds, ready to storm it. Me and a fewscore of other white liberals had put our bodies in between, holding hands with each other, armed blacks behind us and armed cops in front . . . it was scary as hell, but there was playacting involved too, a big American psychodrama, the college president and the blacks' leader were up on a stage together at the end, hugging each other, I don't quite see that happening here. God, I'm hungry. Do you want some muesli?

He goes to the sack and spoons some into a bowl.

Ruth   You don't know what's been happening here.

What the people have gone through. How could you?
You got out.

Peter   Why are the police not intervening, this is
wholesale lawlessness . . . why are the Army standing
aside, watching people being roughed up, vehicles being
hijacked, shops being looted, doing sod-all about it?
Who's supposed to be in charge?

Ruth   They can't take on an entire community. You
don't know your own people, not any more. This strike
is theirs. They're completely behind it now. Nationalist
rebels have been imposed as executive ministers, ruling
over them, against their will . . .

Peter   Do us a favour . . .

Ruth   They won't be coerced. They won't be dictated
to. All they're proving is what your sort was always
chanting – the power lies with the people. Only in this
case it's your own people. You have no notion how they
feel, you opted out. You lost touch. You see it all like
the English now, 'a plague on both their houses' . . .
easy to say when it isn't your own house that's in mortal
danger.

Peter   I haven't exactly noticed you manning the
barricades.

Ruth   There's no shortage of volunteers.

Peter   And this is what your husband makes of it all?

Ruth   My husband and I are separated.

Peter   He hasn't tracked you down yet, then?

Ruth   I wrote. Told him – not to bother.

She bites her lip, fighting back the tears.

Peter   That's the stuff. (*Proffering the bowl of muesli.*) Have
some of this.

Ruth   No thanks.

Peter (*pouring milk on the muesli*) Just the powdered milk, I'm afraid. Go ahead. (*She shakes her head.*) Sure? (*He shovels a spoonful into his mouth, munches it.*) It's not bad at all, actually. (*He takes another spoonful.*) Aaggh! (*He clutches his jaw in pain, thrusting the muesli bowl aside.*)

Ruth   What's up?

Peter   Bugger it.

Ruth   Broken filling?

Peter   All I need.

Ruth   It's those wee black things. (*Looking in the bowl.*) Lenny says it's buckshot.

Peter   They're seeds.

Ruth   Do you want an aspirin? He says he read it on the packaging . . .

Peter   Buck*wheat*!

Ruth   How did you find such a big bag of that stuff?

Peter   American couple, downstairs. Made it up for me.

Ruth   You mean in Birmingham?

Peter   They have a health-food shop. Under my flat.

Ruth   It's tasteless muck, isn't it.

Peter   Well, it hasn't been fried sodden, in rancid lard, if that's what you mean. So it scarcely counts as fit to eat at all, in this wee province of ours.

Ruth   You don't think very much of us, do you.

Peter   Why can I never remember it, until the minute I set foot . . . that ache in the arse, whatever the direct opposite of homesickness is. Exilephilia. The desperate nagging pain of longing to be far, far away.

Ruth   In Birmingham, you mean? Do you really like it there?

Peter   It's a lot bigger.

Ruth   It's where all the roads are, isn't it.

She goes into the kitchen and fetches him a glass of water and two aspirin.

Here. Take these.

Peter (*taking the glass*)   What are we supposed to do when they turn this stuff off?

Ruth   I've already filled up every receptacle in the house.

Peter   Amazing . . .

Ruth   We'll get by fine. Sooner or later the English will cave in, they have to. They'll disband the executive.

Peter   Out of the whole four of us – you're the only one who's really coping with all this.

Ruth   I just like having things to do. Looking after people. At school I always wanted to be a nurse, really bad . . .

Peter   The uniform would suit you.

Ruth   Only trouble being, it's the sort of thing you need a good stomach for.

Peter   Looks terrific from here.

Ruth   No, I mean, you know what I mean, not the uniform. Blood and things. Not my strong point. I've always been quite well organised, though.

Peter   Lucky somebody is, in this house.

Ruth   Is it really bad? The tooth?

Peter   A slight throb, that's all. Sorry I blew a fuse earlier.

Ruth   Don't mention it.

Peter   Kiss and make up, then.

Ruth   That's right.

Peter   I've been meaning to ask you, how did you and Marian come to be friends?

Ruth   The swimming.

Peter   What swimming?

Ruth   We both swam for our schools, we got selected for the Northern Ireland youth squad. We went away to Scotland and Holland. She was nearly seventeen, I was only thirteen, I wasn't like you, I was desperately homesick, it used to be the buses and trams that set me off the worst – the funny colour of them, I cried my eyes out over that. Honest to God, the things you feel. I'm no different, even now. Anyhow. It was Marian looked after me, she was like a big sister. We just somehow stayed friends, from that day to this.

Peter   It must be the swimming that keeps your figure so lithe.

Ruth   Oh, I don't compete now . . . not since my marriage . . . just for the club occasionally . . . you see, David, my husband, he was a real championship swimmer, I met him then too.

Peter   Lucky fellow.

Ruth   Not in his book.

Peter   You must have been spoilt for choice, with your looks.

Ruth   Oh, yes. Fighting them off.

Peter   Bet you were.

Ruth   Some hope.

Peter   You're quite remarkable, Ruth. In my book,

that is.

Ruth   Not me.

Peter   Can I ask you something?

Ruth   Up to you.

Peter   It may seem a bit presumptuous.

Ruth   What is it?

Peter   Supposing we really were to kiss and make up?

Ruth   What sort of a question's that . . .

He's kissing her. Slowly and tentatively, she begins to respond. He guides her to the sofa, sits her down, lifts her legs on to the sofa so that she is lying with her knees bent, and him kneeling by her. He kisses her again, gently nudging her skirt up over her knees, and caressing her thighs. The sound of **Lenny***'s solo trombone suddenly blares out from upstairs.* **Ruth** *thrusts* **Peter** *aside and sits up.*

Ruth   What's he doing here?

Peter   They were both supposed to be searching for the car.

Ruth   He must have been dossing up there this whole time, he could easy have been in on us!

She is hurriedly pulling down her skirt and sitting up straight.

Peter   Easy, it's all right, we'll go into the front parlour.

Ruth   We can't do that, not in there.

Peter   There's a lock on the door.

Ruth   Lily always kept it special!

Peter   It's a room, that's all. It's privacy.

Ruth   Marian would kill me!

Peter   Ruth, it's our business. It's strictly between us.

Our secret. You and me.

He strokes her hair, gently kisses her again. Then he takes the candle and leads her by the hand, out the hall door and towards the forbidden pleasures of the front parlour. **Lenny**'s *trombone continues for a while from upstairs. There is a sudden hammering from outside the backyard door.* **Marian**'s *voice is heard shouting 'Lenny! Lenny! Hello! Down here! Open up!' The trombone music stops and* **Lenny** *is heard thundering down the stairs: he appears, rushing in from the hall carrying a torch, and continues straight through the kitchen to the scullery door, which he unlocks and opens; and thence down the yard to the yard door which he unbolts and flings back – to reveal* **Marian**, *in the light of the torch, mud-spattered with her coat ripped, and scratch marks on her face. She makes straight for the kitchen to wash her face and hands, while he re-bolts and re-locks the two doors.*

Lenny   Are you hurt bad?

Marian   Scratched a bit, but not as much as my car is.

Lenny   You found it?

Marian   It's the centrepiece of the barricade at the entrance to the estate up there.

Lenny   I suppose it's where we should have looked first.

Marian   There wasn't anybody about, I tried to drive it away.

Lenny   Chrissake, Marian, that was totally asking for it!

Marian   They knew me instantly on sight of course – 'that Fenian hoor of a squatter' – that's what they actually think we are – squatters.

Lenny   Right.

Marian   It's quite funny, actually.

Lenny   That's it. We're moving out.

Marian   It was all women – shrieking and squealing and scrabbing at me, is that your radio? (*She has just spotted it on the table.*)

Lenny   We can camp out in my place ...

Marian   I thought I told you to keep it out of here. (*Thrusting the radio into his midriff.*)

Lenny   Where's Ruth and Peter? (*Registering the radio.*) Whose is this?

Marian   Yeah, take him and her with you both. If you walk across town you should have no problems.

Lenny   We'll leave together, all four of us.

Marian   I'm the one who lives here, if you recall. I'm going nowhere, I've only just got home.

Lenny   Marian, we're not talking personal issues, not any longer. This right here is Nazi Belfast now, and it's us playing the Jews.

Marian   God, but you're simple. People, cast adrift, in hysterics ... spare me your vision of the Third Reich in Ballyhackamore.

Lenny   Look at yourself. Look at the news. It's nearly two weeks now, the animals have taken over the zoo, it's all poised on the verge of a massive pogrom, we're sitting here like a row of ducks in a shooting gallery.

Marian *has been getting out a big church candle from a drawer and lighting it, to supplement the light from the camping lamp left behind by* **Ruth** *and* **Peter**.

Marian   Sounds to me like you haven't got a minute to lose.

Lenny   Right, okay. I'm withdrawing the house from sale.

Marian   Ruth's car is still sitting up there, untouched, up in the churchyard, if you want to try using that. You better go and get your gear together, there's a good boy.

Lenny   The contracts are off. Null and void.

Marian   Yes, well away you and explain all that to your Uncle Phelim, if you can track him down in his underground bunker, it's somewhere up Fortwilliam way, isn't that right?

Lenny   What exactly do you envisage happening here – the National Trust turning up in riot gear and storming the house to rescue you?

Marian   I'm seeing this through. That's all. On my own terms. For Jesus' sake just leave me in peace, the whole shower of you, I'm sick of your filth and mess and noise and bickering, in every last corner of the house, I've had enough.

Lenny   Marian . . .

Marian   You find a refuge, you find a task for your life, and then wholesale panic breaks out, and they all come crowding in the door, her and you and that trend-worshipping narcissist . . .

Lenny   It's beside the point, you're in terrible danger, we've all got to get out of here. The last thing I ever intended or needed, me and you under the same roof, it was another one of his lame jokes, (*Gesturing skywards.*) okay, we move out, we go our separate ways to our respective families. I don't like to see you in the state you're in. You're just not fit to be left on your own.

Marian *slowly turns on him.*

Marian   What are you getting at?

Lenny   I'm talking about what's going on!

Marian   Such as?

Lenny What have we been having this entire conversation about?

Marian You consider that I'm cracking up?

Lenny When did I say that?

Marian Not fit to be alone?

Lenny In this house, that's all!

Marian It wouldn't maybe have occurred to you, it wouldn't maybe have penetrated even that dim featherweight brain – that being on my own is the one thing I am fit for?

Lenny Okay ...

Marian That being on my own is precisely what I bought this house for, the reason I sold my business and my flat, the reason I reconciled myself to meeting you for an evening to look this place over?

Lenny Okay, okay, but it's all changed – out there!

Marian It's all changed in here, Lenny. For five weeks you've been living with me again. It took me three years to break out of our marriage, and now for the past five weeks you've been living with me again, here in this house, the very place I chose as a refuge. So even if you do believe that I'm cracking up ...

Lenny I never said you were cracking up ...

Marian ... it's conceivably not actually a psychiatrist that I need ...

Lenny Who said you needed a psychiatrist?

Marian You've always been very ready with that solution in the past.

Lenny For pity's sake, Marian ...

Marian It may just be that all I need is to get the three spineless parasites, with whom I'm presently saddled, off my back – or maybe your uncle the psychiatrist would consider such a desire irrational?

Lenny Quit it, will you, just scrub it, it's the same old trick all over, putting words into my mouth to avoid facing your own reality . . .

Marian Don't start the usual bloody put-upon whinge. I'm not one of your doting maiden aunts, I can see clean through it, you can't face up to emotion in any shape or form . . .

Lenny Here it comes.

Marian Feeling. Passion. This. (*Jabbing at her heart.*) Every time I stubbed my toe or smashed a tumbler and swore loudly, you were offering to turn me over to your uncle the psychiatrist, it's beyond your capability, grown-up anger, pain, commitment, love – have you never considered that if one of us needs treatment it might be you?

Lenny I never know how you do this, I start off trying to help you, and within ten minutes I'm a villain, I'm a deviant, I'm the one in need of help, in the name of God just face reality!

Marian Which reality did you have in mind?

Lenny Your own, Marian, your own reality, you've been talking to yourself, you've been counting spoons, you've been babbling in tongues in the middle of the night!

Too late he realises the blunder. Now that she has successfully accomplished it, **Marian** *relaxes.*

Marian Thanks, Lenny. Very much. I thought we were never going to get to it.

Lenny Well, what are we *supposed* to think?

Marian Don't think, Lenny. Don't think anything at all. Don't even try. It doesn't agree with you. Here's

what we're doing. I'm staying here with my tongues –
and you're going home with your trombone. That way
we're all quits. Okay?

Lenny I don't know why I waste my time. You'd
think I'd know better by now.

He retires, out the hall door and back up the stairs. **Marian**
closes the door after him. **Lily Matthews** *immediately appears
from the shadows of the pantry. She is wearing the print dress now
without the pinafore over it, and her hair is down: we can see in
her the ghost of her thirty-three-year-old self.*

Lily Nice way to treat your own husband.

Marian Lenny's no husband of anybody's. Never was,
never will be.

Lily In the eyes of God he's your man still.

Marian God's eyes were put out, Lily, did you not
hear.

Lily What sort of talk is that?

Marian The old boy. Blinded. He only exists in the
dark now.

Lily Have you drink taken?

Marian We're his guide dogs now. Dragging him
round from pillar to post. Half of us in rut, and the
other half rabid. Without us, he can't survive. But
without him, without him, to love, honour and obey . . .
it's just a dog's life for us. So far as I can see.

Lily Is this the sort of blasphemous babble the priests
are filling your heads with now?

Marian What makes you think I'm a Catholic?

Lily I suppose that's your idea of amusement.
Sacrilege and mockery.

Marian You're out in your figure today, I see. Where

did you get that dress from, anyway?

Lily   Mind your own business.

Marian   The height of the Depression, Alfie two years jobless . . . it was Alan Ferris bought it for you, wasn't it?

Lily   What if it was, he was a good lodger and a good friend to us.

Marian   The English airman. Stores and maintenance, Sydenham aerodrome.

Lily   It was only him spied it, that was the reason. Hanging in Price's window. He egged me on to try it on for size, it was my birthday, that was why. Before I know where I am, he's the money out and paid across the counter, and me walking out of the shop still wearing it. When he was in one of those daft oul' moods of his, he could charm the birds down out of the trees.

Marian   Crêpe-de-Chine.

Lily   I never owned anything like that in my life before, the sheer clean feel of it all over you . . .

Marian   Did you go dancing?

Lily   I was a married woman of thirty-three, catch yourself on.

Marian   You went to Groomsport, though.

Lily   Who told you that?

Marian   I'm thirty-three as well, Lily.

Lily   What of it?

Marian   Did you make a day of it?

Lily   No, we did not, his skin was very fair, he burnt easy, he didn't like the sand. It was only an evening dander along the front. The sun was setting over the lough, hanging out of the sky like a big swollen blood orange. The water all glistening with the redness of it and the sky and the hills on fire with it. Like what you'd see after a war, maybe ... it took your breath away, it was a real picture, but it was frightening. That's what I thought anyhow.

Marian   Did you say it?

Lily   He laughed. Nothing frightened him.

Marian   Why would it.

Lily   We stood there and looked, at the water, and the air. He'd come from across the water, you see. Flown across, through the air. I'd never even been on the water, let alone up in the air, couldn't imagine it. I wanted to. It was frightening, but. We just stood there and looked, in the cool of the evening, drinking it in.

Marian   I could do with an evening in Groomsport myself, just at the minute.

She sits down in the rocking-chair.

Lily   All we did was stand and look, across the water.

Marian   That was the moment when it hit you, though. You already could tell that he wanted you. That was the moment you realised that you were going to give yourself ... all of yourself, whatever he wanted to do to you, that same evening ...

Lily   Keep you your guttersnipe mind to yourself, what do you know about my life, over forty years ago!

Marian   Only what I've read, Lily.

She reaches into the raffia basket which is tucked in beside the rocking-chair, and takes out an old and disintegrating leather-bound padlocked diary.

Lily   How did you get hold of that?

Marian   Under the cellar stairs wasn't the ideal place

for it. There's dampness there. Mildew. Rust. The lock
has rusted away, look.

She holds up the diary and it swings open, the lock coming adrift.

Lily Leave that be, that's private property, don't you
dare touch that!

Marian You wanted it read, Lily, you must have.

Lily No!

Marian Why else hide it? Why write it? You wanted
somebody to know. It's just turned out to be me, that's
all.

Lily Why can't you mind your own business, what
right have you to go poking and prying into a body's
private life . . .

Marian What about the life of your baby?

Lily My baby was strong . . . he was well happed-
up . . .

Marian You abandoned him.

Lily I entrusted him to the care of the Lord!

Marian You left him lying in the porch of a Baptist
church!

Lily A well-off congregation, it was for the best . . .
moneyed people . . . some pair of them would take him
in, adopt him as their own, what did you want me to
do, he had a better chance there than the orphanage or
the hospital . . .

Marian He would have had his best chance right
here, being reared by you and Alfie.

Lily My Alfie would have struck the pair of us down
dead. He was capable of it, he knew it too, he told me
the day we moved in here, never make me lose my
temper . . . he never found out, about the child, that

was the one mercy, he was away that whole year
tramping all over England, looking for work with Jackie
Midgely. Nobody ever knew but me, my own mother
was dead by then with the TB, I was inclined towards
stoutness then anyway . . . one day it just arrived . . . on
that floor, five hours I lay there . . . I delivered it myself.
By the time Alfie come home again, the whole thing
was over and done, as though it had never been . . . he
had no inkling of any of it, from then till his dying day.

Marian You and Alan Ferris. On the front parlour
sofa. He'd no inkling of that?

Lily Oh, sweet God in heaven forgive me!

Marian Alfie was impotent, wasn't he. A souvenir of
Passchendaele, maybe. Scarcely the first nor the last to
come back from the dead in that condition.

Lily I sinned against my own flesh in lust and
fornication, I had to desert my own baby, nobody ever
knew only the Lord our God knew and His eye was on
me all right, burning into the very soul of me, He alone
was witness to the torment that I've suffered every living
hour in this house where the very walls and doors cry
out against me, there was never anybody to tell the
knife that went through me a dozen dozen times a day,
minding how I left my child, walking away from him,
leaving him bundled up there in that wooden box,
nobody to help me, only me here in this house, gnawing
and tearing away at my own heart and lights, day in
day out . . . until I was all consumed by my own
wickedness, on the inside, nothing left but the shell of
me, for appearance's sake . . . still and all. At least I
never let myself down – never cracked. Never
surrendered. Not one inch. I went to my grave a
respectable woman, Mrs Alfred George Matthews, I
never betrayed him. That was the way I atoned, you
see. I done him proud. He never knew any reason to be
ashamed of me, or doubt my loyalty. From the day we

met till the day I went to my grave.

Marian You loved Alan Ferris, Lily. These things can't be helped. He introduced you to the body's actual passion. The English airman. Then he flew away.

Lily Alan ... he came from across the water, you see ... there was a picture in my Bible, at Sunday school, the fair-skinned archangel standing at the gates of heaven, that was what he looked like ... only he was a dark angel. Angel of death. Agent of Satan. He swept me up, high up, took me up into the sky ... and then he dropped me. Left me. Flew home. Left me falling. Falling.

Marian *takes* **Lily**'s *hand and holds it against her own heart.*

Marian Forgive me, Lily.

Lights fade to blackout.

Scene Two

The early hours of Sunday, 2 June. **Marian** *is asleep on the sofa in the dark kitchen. There is a glimmering of distant bonfires in the night sky above the yard, and the faint sounds of an Orange band playing and of a mob celebrating. Gradually this is overtaken by the din of a military helicopter approaching and hovering low over the house.* **Peter** *appears outside, dragging himself up on to the top of the yard wall, having climbed up from a dustbin in the alley on the far side. He has a banjo case slung across his back. He is suddenly caught in the blinding searchlight of the hovering helicopter. He shields his eyes from the light with an arm.* **Marian**, *awakened by this, goes to the window.* **Peter** *drops down into the yard and makes for the scullery door.* **Marian** *goes to it and lets him in. The searchlight switches off and the helicopter moves away.* **Marian** *is lighting the gas mantles as* **Peter** *talks.*

Peter Couldn't get back into the street ... just young

bloods drunk, dozens of them, hooligan types. I was carrying a couple of bottles, you see, they probably thought it was whiskey or something, they'd a shock in store, it was my father's elderberry wine. You wouldn't exactly want to die for it, Christ . . . I'm all slashed on that wall. At least I managed to hang on to my old banjo. Cold, isn't it. Sorry to disturb you. I hadn't expected, what with the strike being over, I see the gas supply has returned anyway . . .

Marian   Not to mention the Army.

Peter   What? Oh, right, right, the chopper, yeah, I was actually bloody glad, as a matter of fact, it showing up. At least it got them off my back . . .

Marian   There's a glimmer of life in that fire. Hoke it out and throw those sticks on it.

She exits to the bathroom to fetch the first-aid kit. **Peter,** *alone and shivering, goes to the press where the remains of the drink are stored and takes a swig of vodka.* **Ruth** *rushes in, in her nightdress.*

Ruth   Marian says you were attacked . . .

Peter   I'm fine.

Ruth   You poor love, you're all cut . . .

Peter *thrusts his bloodstained hand in front of her face.*

Peter   Oh yeah, the red hand. Makes you puke, doesn't it. Blood and things.

He turns away from her and tends to the fire.

Ruth   I'm only trying to be your friend, Peter.

Marian *returns with* **Lily**'s *first-aid box.*

Peter   I'll let you both get back to sleep, then.

Marian   Sit down.

Peter   I'll just go and get myself cleaned up . . . (*But* *she has firmly planted him in the chair and is starting to swab the cuts on his hands.*) ... ah. Well. Thanks. Funny time for this, isn't it. They're all celebrating, out there. My crowd and hers, I mean. The end of being forced to share the top table with a few Popeheads, they're beside themselves with the glorious deliverance of it, the executive forced to resign, you'd think they'd given birth, actually created something for once, instead of battering it to death, yet again, the only kind of victory they ever credit, holding the good old fort, stamping the life out of anything that starts to creep forward, even my reverend father and mother were quietly crowing over it, in the same way she is of course, (*At* **Ruth**.) with a proper air of restrained well-balanced smugness ...

Ruth   Stop it!

Peter   What odds, they're all one, under the skin, all at one with those vicious little buggers, out there, who put their toecaps into me ... (*He suddenly breaks down but immediately swallows it back.*) ... sorry, I don't know ...

Marian   It's this stuff, it shows no mercy.

Peter   I don't, I don't know why it matters, why I care, I don't know, what the fuck I have to come back here for, what I expect, what it is I think I'll find here, whatever it is I think I'm missing ...

Lenny *comes in from the hall, returning from a gig, in his street clothes and carrying his trombone.*

Lenny   What's going on, then?

Ruth   Peter got roughed up.

She brushes out past him.

Lenny (*to* **Peter**)   I thought you were visiting your parents?

Peter   Correct.

Lenny   What happened?

Peter   Who knows – my mother just suddenly went for my hands with a broken bottle.

Lenny   Your mother's a Justice of the Peace!

Marian *is finishing cleaning the cuts on* **Peter**'s *hands and putting plaster on them.*

Peter (*to* **Marian**)   Did he ever tell you how close we came to preventing the entire Ulster conflict from getting off the ground?

Marian   Bound to have.

Lenny   You're not referring to McManus, I hope?

Marian   Bound to be.

Ruth *re-enters wearing a dressing gown.*

Peter   There was a spaceman we all knew, as students, you see, Ruth – a wild mad bugger called Vincent Moog McManus, he stayed on indefinitely as a research student in chemistry. (**Lenny** *has retreated to the kitchen to fetch himself a scrap of food.*) He spent most of his time in the lab synthesising LSD – the drug, that is – and I'm not talking in spoonfuls, he had rows of big sweety jars lined along his kitchen shelves, chocolate éclairs, liquorice comfits, you name it, all fully primed. This was high-class stuff, before anybody here had even heard tell of it, Moog was a bona-fide visionary. So one hot night, pinhead here and me and Moog were tripped out in my garden, beatific, except there'd been the early riots, the initial killings, the first stirrings of the reawakening of the Protestant dragon and the Catholic dragon, and the three of us felt a messianic impulse, to slay these ancient monsters, we felt summoned, as a holy trinity of the new age, father son and holy ghost, Moog being the ghost and me the messiah, but it was Godhead here who came up with the redemption – why not take the total stash of acid in Moog's sweety jars, transport it up to the Mourne Mountains, and dump it into the Silent

Valley reservoir? The entire Belfast water supply was in that lovely man-made lake. We could turn on the population, comprehensively, with one simple transcendental gesture, that would be it, the doors of perception flung wide, wholesale mind-shift, no more bigotry and hatred, a city full of spaced-out contemplatives like the three of us. So off I went and filched the keys of my mother's Austin Princess, and we loaded it up with the sweety jars and headed for the hills. We actually got as far as Dundrum . . . before negative signals began to filter through even to us, scrambled brains and all, we hadn't seen the news, not for days, that was the basic flaw. The Silent Valley reservoir had been blown up by the UVF. Belfast was dry. The Mourne Mountains were swarming like an anthill with the security forces. We got searched three times on the way home . . . Moog said he was a supplier for his family's confectionery business, it was true in a way, not that it made any odds, they wouldn't have known the drug if we'd force-fed them on it, we were entirely beside the point, am I right, head? What the hell. At least we tried. How many can say as much.

Lenny *has registered the banjo.*

Lenny Is that your old five-string?

Peter Haven't played it in five years.

Lenny How's the tuning?

Peter You tell me.

Lenny *removes the banjo from its case and quietly tunes it up during the ensuing dialogue.*

Peter So anyway, there you go. That's my bedtime story. Time for you three girls to kiss and tell. Seeing as we're all up and about. What do you say, Marian? How about dishing the real dirt on Orange Lily Matthews, you must have dug up some scandal by this time.

Marian   I found a used condom behind the parlour sofa. (*An awkward moment all round.*) The pair of you might have cleaned up behind you, at least.

Peter   I don't think much of that, as a story.

Ruth   I really am sorry, Marian . . .

Marian   I'll give you a story. Lily sat in that parlour, right through the Blitz. Alfie was a fire warden, out most nights – she promised him she'd stay down in the cellar during the air-raids, instead of which she sat up in that front parlour, in the blackout, the pitch dark, listening to the war in the air . . . the bombers and the fighters, the ack-ack and the shells falling, falling and exploding . . . she stretched out on that self-same sofa, where Alan Ferris had stretched her out seven years earlier and pleasured her till her ears sang with a whole wild uncontainable babble . . .

Peter   Holy shit, tell us more.

Lenny   Quiet.

Marian   She lay down in the dark on her own now, and pictured him, up there, burning a hole through the sky, a dark angel, and her ears roared now with the rage of a wholesale slaughter, pounding the ground under her and the air all round her, Armageddon, random and blind, pulverising her whole body until she once more came and came again, and she composed herself to die there, waiting for the chosen bomb to fall on her and cleanse her terrible sinfulness and shame . . . the street next to this one was totally flattened one night. The parlour windows came in on her, but Lily wasn't even scratched. The skies cleared. The war ended. And there she still was – unscathed. She interpreted this as her punishment. She had been condemned to life. A life sentence.

They are all reduced to silence, staring into the fire.

Lenny   I wonder what it was like here. Before Christianity.

Ruth   What are you going to do with the house, Marian?

Marian   Live in it.

Peter   National Trust permitting, you mean.

Marian   That was a wrong impulse. A mistaken idea. It would only have been perpetuating a crime . . . condemning her to life indefinitely. I'm clearing most of this out. Keeping just the basics. Fixing it up. What this house needs most is air and light.

She starts building up the fire with turf.

Peter   Exactly what I say. Minor gentrification . . . (*To* **Lenny**.) As for you, head, you appear to be saying nothing.

Lenny   What of it?

Peter   It's your turn for the story.

Lenny (*offering him the banjo*)   Here, you're in tune now.

Peter   You play it, I think I've lost my touch. (*Holding up his hands.*) Give us a talking blues.

Lenny *fools around on the banjo for a moment.*

Lenny   There was something happened to me last summer – as it happens – last August, down near Kinsale. (*He sets the banjo aside.*) There's a Dutch guy with a pub there, runs a lot of jazz nights. This particular night went on till half-six in the morning, the sun was hanging out, I was ready for a look at the ocean, so was the lady vocalist. She was a strange woman, half gipsy, from Sligo or somewhere weird like that, totally wrecked on everything on offer, which was plenty . . . so. We stumbled down to this cove, a lovely horseshoe of sand, except her and me couldn't handle any more bright

lights, so we collapsed on to a sheltered bit of grass
behind some boulders. And your woman starts crooning.
(*Sings.*) 'Just a closer walk with thee . . .' lying there
splayed out in the warm singing away . . . and she
begins to peel her clothes off. Nothing to do with me –
she was stretched out flat with her eyes closed – but
before too long, she's entirely bare, the voice floating in
the early breeze, (*Sings.*) 'Grant it Jesus if you please . . .',
and I'm hunkered down beside her, with a swollen
mouth from playing all night, staring out at the glittery
water, stunned all over, the way you are. And then, into
my line of vision – there comes this sight, at first I
thought I was hallucinating, it was a gaggle of nuns, real
nuns, in the whole gear, which they were busy stripping
off, over their heads. There was a dozen or more of
them. It was a nuns' swimming party. Underneath their
habits, they had these interlock jobs, sort of vests and
baggy long johns. I suppose they reckoned at that hour
there'd be nobody to see them. So down they pelted
into the sea, frisking around and frolicking like nine-
year-olds, the noise of it – while your woman is
meanwhile stretched out starkers beside me, singing this
deep-throated heartfelt version of 'Just a Closer Walk
With Thee' . . . entirely oblivious . . . and the nuns are
splashing each other, and giggling and screaming, and
flinging themselves about in the golden light, with the
wet interlock clinging to their excited bodies – and it
doesn't take a lot to see that the nuns are experiencing
their sex and the vocalist her spirit. And for a crazy few
seconds I all but sprinted down to the nuns to churn my
body into theirs, in the surf foam, and then bring them
all back to the lady vocalist, for a session of great
spirituals . . . and maybe that's how it was . . . what it
was like here. Before Christianity. Is what I'm saying.

Ruth   You don't even know Christianity. You think it's
only denial, but that's wrong. It's meant to be love and
celebration. You don't even know what day it is now,
the meaning of it.

Peter   You tell them, Ruthie child. Pentecost Sunday.

Lenny   So what? (*He has turned away from this to his trombone, which he takes out and cleans and puts together.*)

Ruth   The day our Lord's apostles were inspired by the Holy Spirit. 'And when the day of Pentecost was fully come, they were all with one accord in one place. And suddenly there came a sound from heaven as of a rushing mighty wind, and it filled all the house where they were sitting. And there appeared unto them cloven tongues like as of fire, and it sat upon each of them. And they were all filled with the Holy Ghost, and began to speak with other tongues, as the Spirit gave them utterance.' (*She retreats into herself again.*)

Peter   You can't stop there. It's your story, you have to finish it.

Ruth   I don't remember it all.

Peter   'And they were all amazed, and were in doubt, saying to one another, What meaneth this? . . .'

Ruth   'Others mocking said, These men are full of new wine . . .'

Peter   'But Peter, standing up with the eleven, lifted up his voice and said unto them: Ye men of Judea and all ye that dwell at Jerusalem, let this be known unto you and hearken to my words: For these are not drunken as ye suppose, seeing it is but the third hour of the day . . .'

Ruth (*squaring up to him, as it turns into a contest*)   'But this is that which was spoken by the prophet Joel: And it shall come to pass in the last days, saith God, I will pour out of my spirit upon all flesh: and your sons and your daughters shall prophesy, and your young men shall see visions, and your old men shall dream dreams. And on my servants and on my handmaidens I will

pour out in those days of my spirit; and they shall
prophesy . . .'

Peter 'And I will shew wonders in heaven above, and
signs in the earth beneath; blood and fire, and vapour of
smoke; the sun shall be turned into darkness, and the
moon into blood, before that great and notable day of
the Lord come . . .'

Ruth 'And it shall come to pass, that whosoever shall
call on the name of the Lord shall be saved.'

Peter The old familiar payoff! – but it hasn't entirely
held up, Ruthie. I mean they're never done calling on
the name of the Lord in this wee province of ours, so it
ought to be the most saved place on God's earth instead
of the most absolutely godforsaken, not so?

Ruth Some of us love this province.

Peter By God you do and with a vengeance, and
you've finally loved it to death, Ruth, stone dead and in
its grave and we're all sitting here at the wake. Take a
long hard look. Because our whole wee family's here,
gathered together round the hearth, our *holy* family –
Marian the mother at the head, the holy virgin,
shielding us from all harm, keeping faithful little Ruthie
safe from her night fears, the funny-coloured buses and
the psychopathic Christian spouse . . .

Ruth Leave you David out of this, you're not worth a
hair of his head!

Peter We're certainly not in any doubt that you'll be
going back to him.

Ruth He's up in Purdysburn Hospital, if you must
know.

Marian What happened?

Ruth He's had a breakdown. Smashed his own two
hands to a pulp before they could restrain him.

Marian You never told me, Ruth.

Ruth I went to visit him. Told him it was over. He's accepted it. He knows I won't be going back.

Peter Why not? I thought you were hell-bent on being a nurse.

Lenny All right, enough! No more.

Marian Leave him. Let him get rid of it.

Peter You see how she forgives the one stray sheep, the prodigal, we're such an Irish little family, the strong saintly suffering ma and the shiftless clown of a da here, no damn use to man or beast, hunched up against the wall, hands in empty pockets, jiggling his limp thing like a dead hen's thrapple . . .

Lenny No more of this shit tonight . . .

Peter *grabs hold of him.*

Peter Pentecost is upon us, head, so where's the fire on your tongue? Or is there maybe not a fizzle left in any part of you at all?

Lenny Not like you, I suppose, dicking your way round the Brummie discos every night of the week . . .

Peter You're never going to leave here, face it, your life's locked in and the key surrendered . . .

Lenny I'll live whatever life I choose, and I'll live it here, what's it to you, you think you're any further on? You seriously think I'd want what you have? I live like a prince compared to you, I live for my real friends, for good crack, I'm a musician, I live for what I play!

Peter On that? (*The trombone.*) Play on that? You want to know what playing on that is? Farting into the wind.

Lenny, *with a sudden spasm of rage, dislodges* **Peter**'*s grip on him, flings him across the table, and then turns away in self-disgust.*

Peter (*winded, picking himself up*) Of course . . . we're null

and void as a holy family, aren't we ... missing our
most important member ... the Prince of Peace
Himself. (*Pulling himself painfully into a seat.*) Can you see
him? Here? Can you see him? Dandering down Royal
Avenue? Dropping into a council meeting at the City
Hall? The Son of Man ... in the middle of the
marching ranks of the Ulster zealots, watching at the
elbow of the holy Catholic Nationalist zealot as he puts
a pistol to a man's knee, to a man's brains, to a man's
balls, the Son of God in the polling booth, observing the
votes being cast in support of that, suffering the little
children with murder festering in their hearts, what
would Jesus Holy Christ do with us all here, would you
say?

Lenny I'll tell you exactly what he'd do, he'd close
down every church and chapel, temple and tabernacle in
the whole island, put them to the torch, burn them into
rubble, turf the congregations out priests and pastors
face first, and drive them up into the mountains, up to
the boniest, bleakest stretches of the Sperrins and the
Mournes, and he'd flay them into the rock, until the
Christianity was scourged out of the very marrows of
their bones, he'd expunge religion once and for all from
off the face of this country, until the people could
discover no mercy except in each other, no belief except
to believe in each other, no forgiveness but what the
other would forgive, until they cried out in the dark for
each other and embraced their own humanity ... that's
the only redemption he'd offer them. Never mind
believing in Jesus Christ. That's the point at which Jesus
Christ might just begin to believe in us.

Peter Why would he come near the place, let's face it,
he's already been crucified once. He's already been once
in hell.

Lenny The Church invented hell. They've just used
this town to show us what they mean.

Marian They. They. You think you can both shuffle
it off, so easily, with your righteous anger, let me tell
you, you're not even in the same league as I am for
righteous anger, I've supped on precious little else for
five years past, it changes nothing. Forget the church.
Forget the priests and pastors. There is some kind of
christ, in every one of us. (**Peter** *and* **Lenny** *turn their
faces against this language.*) Each of us either honours him,
or denies him and violates him, what we do to him is
done to ourselves. I had a child once.

Lenny No. Marian . . .

Marian I called him Christopher. Because he was a
kind of Christ to me, he brought love with him . . . the
truth and the life. He was a future. Until one day I
found him dead. I thought like you for a long time. He
chose death in the cot rather than life in this town, in
these times, it was their fault, they had done it to me, I
hated them. Hated life. It was all a lie, of course. The
cause and effect were in me, in him too, (*At* **Lenny**.) we
were mortal after all, we were human, had to be, we
couldn't bear one another, couldn't tolerate ourselves,
the child was only a fallible mortal the same as us, that
was all that he was telling us. I felt him as a raw scar
across my own spirit, stinging me, every minute, every
hour, everything defaced by it . . . until I was blaming
him, for all the pain, he was one of them too. They. I
denied him. The christ in him. Which he had entrusted
to my care, the ghost of him that I do still carry, as I
carried his little body. The christ in him absorbed into
the christ in me. We have got to love that in ourselves.
In ourselves first and then in them. That's the only
future there is.

She has been on her feet during this, and is close to the sofa where
Lenny *is sitting, hunched up, close to tears now. Privately and
unobtrusively, he touches her hand.*

Personally, I want to live now. I want this house to live.

We have committed sacrilege enough on life, in this place, in these times. We don't just owe it to ourselves, we owe it to our dead too ... our innocent dead. They're not our masters, they're only our creditors, for the life they never knew. We owe them at least that – the fullest life for which they could ever have hoped, we carry those ghosts within us, to betray those hopes is the real sin against the christ, and I for one cannot commit it one day longer.

The sky above the back yard has been growing light. **Lenny,** *overwhelmed by what* **Marian** *has said, picks up his trombone and goes out to the back yard. He sits down on the window ledge.* **Ruth,** *at the table, opens her Bible at the second chapter of the Acts of the Apostles. She reads from it.*

Ruth 'Therefore did my heart rejoice, and my tongue was glad; moreover also my flesh shall rest in hope: Because thou wilt not leave my soul in hell, neither wilt thou suffer thine Holy One to see corruption. Thou hast made known to me the ways of life; thou shalt make me full of joy with thy countenance.'

During this, **Lenny** *has started to play a very slow and soulful version of 'Just a Closer Walk With Thee'. After some time,* **Peter** *picks up his banjo from where it has been left lying, close to him. Tentatively, he starts to pick out an accompaniment to the tune.* **Ruth** *reaches across and opens the window. As the music swells, the lights fade, very slowly, to blackout.*

Printed in the United Kingdom
by Lightning Source UK Ltd.
125852UK00001B/85-183/A